THE MANCHESTER MARTYRS

JOSEPH O'NEILL

MERCIER PRESS
IRISH PUBLISHER – IRISH STORY

MERCIER PRESS

Cork

www.mercierpress.ie

© Joseph O'Neill, 2012

ISBN: 978 1 85635 951 1

10 9 8 7 6 5 4 3 2 1

A CIP record for this title is available from the British Library

Printed and bound in the EU.

CONTENTS

FOR MICK CORRIGAN AND ALL THOSE WHO
HAVE KEPT ALIVE THE MEMORY OF THE
MANCHESTER MARTYRS

The Manchester Martyrs

William Allen
Courtesy of Mercier Archives

Michael Larkin
Courtesy of Mercier Archives

Michael O'Brien
Courtesy of Mercier Archives

INTRODUCTION

The hairs on my arms and neck bristled with the surge of a disquieting emotion. The silence was like none I had ever experienced. Beyond the silence, outside it, was the sound of rain gurgling in the gutters, the relentless Manchester rain falling in great skeins buffeted by the November winds. I was seven years old. It is a moment that will stay with me forever.

Throughout the 1950s, when I was growing up in Manchester, the minute's silence at the spot where the Martyrs died was part of our annual commemoration, a fixture in the calendar of men like my father and many of their children. Together with the Mass, sometimes celebrated by the bishop of Salford, and the prayers at the Martyrs' monument in St Joseph's Cemetery, it did more than forge a bond between the Irish community and the men who, there in our adopted city, died for Irish freedom. Ritual has the power to express the inexpressible. It fashions our hearts.

In the 1960s, however, those who had commemorated the Martyrs became scattered and disparate. The city's programme of slum clearance – the PR men had not yet coined the euphemism 'inner city regeneration' – meant that the wrecking ball smashed the flimsy walls of the cramped houses and pubs once thronged by the nineteenth-century

Manchester Irish. The rubble filled in the old cellars and the rafters and floorboards fed bonfires that lit up the night. The Irish of Moss Side, Hulme, Ancoats and Chorlton-on-Medlock were physically and socially on the move.

Their children, with that chameleon plasticity that marks the Irish wherever they settle, assimilated, the next generation even more. As the conflict in Northern Ireland intensified, commemoration of the Martyrs became, for some, an expression of support for a strident and brutal ideology that invoked past injustices as a rationale for present atrocities. Many saw this development as a subversion of the Martyrs' memory, a misappropriation of the past in the service of current political dogma. The inevitable conflict vitiated the tradition of remembrance and a welter of accusations and counter-accusations drove away most of those who for many years had been the mainstay of the commemoration.

As conflicting groups claimed the legacy of the Martyrs, the events surrounding their execution were forgotten and no one remembered their story. Were they terrorists justly executed for the slaying of a Manchester policeman or were they victims of 'perfidious Albion'? Were they champions of the oppressed working-class, noble bearers of arms in the on-going struggle against international capitalism? Or were they simply Irish republicans, part of an unbroken tradition linking Wolfe Tone to the hunger strikers?[1]

---

1   For more details about the main characters and organisations see Appendix 1.

Unfortunately (or perhaps fortunately) for those who seek to manipulate the past in the service of the present, slogans and rallying cries are crude filters through which to view history. The past remains infuriatingly elusive, nuanced and contradictory and the complexity of people's lives can never be reduced to a war cry. There is far more to the story than its political dimensions.

Certainly, it is a story about political idealism and nationalistic fervour. But it is also about personal bravery, faith and how a group of men prepared themselves to suffer with dignity a public death before a baying crowd eager for any sign of fear. It is about the intrigues of a secret, oath-bound revolutionary conspiracy. It is about one of the most infamous court cases of the nineteenth century. It is about injustice. It is about the fraught relations between England and Ireland. It is about the Irish in England and particularly in the damp, quixotic city of Manchester which has, in equal measure, welcomed us and resented our presence.

I became reacquainted with the story about fifteen years ago and the more I researched the more fascinated I became. Interviews with some of those who had participated in the commemorations, especially Gerry Finn, whose commitment to the memory of the Martyrs over many years gave him a unique insight into the development of the public remembrance, brought me inevitably to the late J. P. (Jimmy) McGill. I had known the latter's bookshops since childhood, without ever realising that he was for decades a moving force in maintaining the commemoration of the Martyrs. Shortly before his death, Jimmy deposited the papers of the Manchester Martyrs Commemoration Committee and related items accumulated over a lifetime, with the Linen Hall Library, Belfast, and it was there that I did a great deal of the research for this book.

Having written many articles and given numerous talks on various aspects of the incident, my brother-in-law suggested that the story was deserving of an accessible account. He provided the first incentive to write this book and over a decade later I acknowledge my debt to him. Since then I have met numerous people in Manchester and Ireland who agree with him and without exception they have been unfailing in their generosity and support, always anxious to share information with me and explain what the Martyrs mean to them.

A Note on Sources

This book is not an academic tome, nor is it a work of fiction. It is a history book written for the general reader who prefers not to have every fact and opinion annotated by reference to obscure sources. It is not a polemic and I hope such views as I express or imply are reasonable. Throughout they are grounded in the evidence and nowhere do they go beyond the known facts. I have sought to step aside and let the story speak for itself. If there are morals or lessons to be drawn from it, I leave you to draw them and confine myself to turning facts into narrative.

Fortunately, there are a great number of relevant facts available, many of them previously unused. Foremost among these are those in the Linen Hall collection, a vast archive of diverse material relating to the Martyrs and their commemoration. It includes booklets, pamphlets, newspaper cuttings and correspondence, together with miscellaneous references to the Martyrs gathered by Jimmy McGill during a lifetime of study.

Newspapers have also proved invaluable sources. Luckily for the historian, Manchester for certain periods in the nineteenth century had up to seven newspapers. Many provide not only verbatim accounts of the court proceedings, but also statements made by a range of interested parties, together with detailed background information about the circumstances under which people were arrested, their appearance, employment and education.

Many of the principal characters also left accounts of these events and Fr Gadd, who ministered to the men while they awaited execution, recorded their reactions during their final days. Many journalists had both access to and contacts within the prison and reported on developments throughout.

Using these and many secondary sources I have sought to construct a narrative which captures the drama inherent in the events while at all times remaining true to the facts.

A NOTE ON DIALOGUE

All the quotations and reported speech in this book are

taken from contemporary newspaper reports, court records or the memoirs and accounts of those directly involved in the events described and other sources. In some cases, particularly in Chapters 8 and 9, I have depicted developments in scenes which involve dialogue. In all cases these scenes are based on the first-hand recollections of those involved and contemporary sources.

PROLOGUE

Calcraft drew the noose tight under Allen's left ear. He could hear the prisoner snorting through the hood covering his head. Allen drew up his shoulders until they touched the noose, as if he would shrug off the rope. The crowd fell silent.

The hangman looked back along the scaffold at the other two hooded figures. O'Brien's shoulders were flung back as if he would face down death. A string of spittle dangled from the hem of Larkin's hood. This is it, Calcraft thought. He drew his hand down from his chin, pulling the white fibres of his beard into a rope.

Fr Gadd took one stride backwards from the drop, but Calcraft stayed, savouring the moment.

'Lord, have mercy. Christ, have mercy,' the priest intoned.

Pushing up against the barriers, the mob strained to see through the mist. The three men shot through the drop. The crowd gasped like a great beast startled.

Calcraft descended the ladder to the pit, his movements deliberate. Before he reached the bottom, he heard the breath rattling in Larkin's throat. The man's tethered legs thrashed as he gurgled.

Calcraft turned to Allen, swaying at the end of the rope,

15

face snapped skywards. With two fingers the hangman touched his shoulder, spinning the body round. Stone dead, his neck snapped like a stick of charcoal.

Larkin's body was still pulsing. Calcraft reached for the rope, drew it to him. Holding Larkin steady, he lifted his foot to the manacle that bound the twitching ankles. Carefully he placed his shoe on the shackle. His body flexing, he leaped up onto the back of the dying man, setting the rope pitching.

Again he levered and jerked, levered and jerked. Tendons popped. Bones cracked. He stepped down, his feet silent on the planks.

'The soldiers are coming,' rose the cry from below, beyond the black drape that hid the drop from the mob. Yelps and shrieks carried up from the street, the clatter of boots and clogs on the cobbles.

Calcraft patted his skullcap. He looked up at O'Brien, whose shoulders still twitched. He'd never seen a man go to the scaffold with such courage. He lifted his leg, ready to jump up on O'Brien's back.

'Leave that man alone!' came a voice from the foot of the ladder. Calcraft turned in disbelief. The priest had appeared without a sound. Before the executioner could speak Fr Gadd advanced towards him, his right arm extended, the black book clutched against his black soutane. His face was as white as his Roman collar.

'He ain't dead, sir. I must finish him off,' protested the old man.

The execution of the Manchester Martyrs
Courtesy of Mercier Archives

'Incompetent buffoon.' The priest's waxy skin was now shot through with rage. 'Get back!' The priest pointed his arm towards the ladder.

The old man's mouth opened. He hesitated. 'I must stay, sir. It's my duty.'

'So long as you keep your hands off him,' said the priest.

Calcraft stepped back, his lips puckered like a scolded child's. He folded his hands behind his back.

Fr Gadd wrapped the chain of the crucifix around O'Brien's fingers and took the other hand in his.

'Take courage, Michael,' he whispered. 'Your loving God has not deserted you. Nor shall I.'

He bent his head in prayer, causing the body to sway:

Out of the depths I cry to You, O Lord!
Lord, hear my voice!
Let your ears be attentive
To the voice of my supplications!

O'Brien groaned.

1

'IRELAND MADE ME'

It takes you by surprise. This part of the cemetery is as fresh and well tended as a military graveyard. Not far from the futuristic museum with its roof like a great axe head suspended in the air, where the paving, slick with rain, runs out, you reach a narrow tarmac path. The smell of damp earth is strong and even in the shelter of the monumental masonry the fitful wind tears at your hair and coat. Then you see it: the first of a Calvary of Celtic crosses. Bolted to the grave fence, which is as tall as a baby's cot, is a heart-shaped plaque bearing the legend 'God Save Ireland'. In the feeble December light the sandstone cross is gunmetal grey. Inscribed on the base are three names and below them, again, 'God Save Ireland'. The grave itself is empty.

Not six strides away is the burial place, marked only by a grave curb, of Jeremiah O'Donovan Rossa. On the other side of the path is a monument to the hunger strikers of 1981.

Here in Glasnevin Cemetery's Republican Plot, where the elaborate headstones speak of a love of country now lost to us, Ireland's past appears as an unbroken tradition of patriotic self-sacrifice. In this place where death is transmuted into imperishable glory, chisel and mallet have fused nationalism and religious faith.

Another empty grave, this one dug in a Kilkenny churchyard in 1848, is part of the story of James Stephens, the man who shaped the lives of so many of those now enshrined in Ireland's nationalist pantheon. If it is possible to say some men's lives were determined by a single year, then Stephens was such a man and the year was 1848. Just as he was to play a major role in Irish history in the years after this crucial pivotal point, he was the product of the nation's development in the decades before that defining year. Ireland's past had shaped James Stephens to such an extent that he could justly claim 'Ireland made me'.

Stephens burned with a profound sense of grievance. Since the Union of 1801, Ireland had been ruled directly from Westminster, where MPs from Kerry and Connemara sat with their counterparts from Cornwall and Kendal. When Stephens was born in 1825, practising his faith, and that of almost the entire population, was not only illegal but entailed social and economic ostracism. It was only with Catholic Emancipation in 1829 that the British government dismantled the Penal Laws – legal prohibitions which made the practice of his faith a crime, restricted his ability to own property and limited his opportunities to move up the social hierarchy.

In his campaigns to achieve Catholic Emancipation, the

man known as The Liberator, Daniel O'Connell, had called 'monster meetings', demonstrations attended by enormous numbers of people with no previous role in the political system or experience of activism. Though committed to non-violent campaigning, O'Connell nevertheless demonstrated the effectiveness of mobilising large numbers of the powerless and impoverished. The significance of this was not lost on Stephens, who was convinced that the poor and those with no voice in politics were not simply an inert and lethargic mass: effective organisation might shape them into a force to drive a revolution.

Though O'Connell was also known as 'the king of the beggars', nothing he did improved the economic plight of the Catholic population during Stephens' formative years. Irish peasants were among the poorest in Europe and their privation appalled foreign visitors. Despite Catholic Emancipation, the land remained largely in the hands of absentee landlords and the descendants of Protestant settlers. As for the bulk of the population, by 1840 forty-five per cent of Irish farms consisted of fewer than five acres and half the population relied on potatoes, with two million entirely dependent on them. Many more eked out a living on miniscule holdings supplemented by work as farm labourers. Such industry as there was, chiefly around Dublin and especially Belfast, was insufficient to sustain a population that remained perilously dependent on an agricultural economy which for decades had teetered on the brink of catastrophe.

The sense of injustice which coursed through Stephens' veins was neither abstract nor theoretical. He didn't construct it from propagandist tracts or works of political philosophy. The evidence for it was all around him, everywhere he turned. It stunted the lives of millions of his compatriots who lived from day to day knowing that their very survival was questionable.

What's more, Stephens' Ireland was in many respects an occupied country. Barracks, manned by the Irish constabulary, an armed police force, and the presence of large numbers of British troops permanently stationed in the country, maintained crown control.

The consequences of Ireland's economic structure and British control became apparent in the 1840s in a manner impossible to ignore. The failure of the potato crop in 1845 and the following years led first to hardship and then to starvation. It threatened the families of millions of small peasant farmers and landless labourers with annihilation. The great hunger of the last European famine – Ireland's greatest calamity since the Black Death of the fourteenth century killed half the population – gnawed deep into the Irish mentality and shaped the country's development for the next century and a half.

The Famine killed a million people and drove another million abroad. From a pre-Famine figure of 8,500,000, Ireland's population, alone of European countries, fell for the next 125 years. Death, terror and depopulation stamped on the mind of every politically aware Irish person the

James Stephens
Courtesy of
Mercier Archives

conviction that Britain was unfit to rule them. The Famine proved, at the very least, that Britain's attitude to Ireland was one of callous indifference. Some nationalists saw it in a more sinister light: it was genocide.

Nor was its impact confined to Ireland. As a child in Liverpool, the sight of those escaping the Famine had a profound effect on the future Fenian, John Denvir. Gaunt and spectral, they stank of poverty and death. Their degradation made an indelible mark on Denvir. 'It will not be wondered,' he wrote in *The Life Story of an Old Rebel*, 'that one who saw these things should feel it a duty stronger than life itself to reverse the system of misgovernment which was responsible.'

What's more, the Famine created the Irish diaspora, to which Stephens was later to attribute such a key role in his strategy for Irish independence. There were Irish people in North America and 'mainland' Britain long before the Famine, but it was the mass exodus fuelled by fear of death that accounts for the fact that today there are seventy million Americans and one in five people in Britain with Irish ancestry. It was this vast body of embittered exiles and their descendants, with their inherited anti-English sentiments, that Stephens sought to harness to the cause of Irish independence.

In 1848, however, when Stephens decided to throw in his lot with a group of idealistic, largely middle-class nationalists, known as Young Ireland, he was still virtually unknown. William Smith O'Brien, a leading figure in the Young Ireland movement, had a national reputation, and Stephens decided to take up arms with him. The group attempted a rising at Ballingarry, County Tipperary, although the result was a few inconsequential skirmishes with the police, contemptuously dismissed by the authorities as 'the Battle of the Widow McCormack's Cabbage Patch'. Stephens was wounded in the thigh and subsequently went to ground, seeking to escape the round-up that followed the incident. To put the authorities off the scent, his friends arranged his funeral and had a coffin buried in a Kilkenny churchyard. The *Kilkenny Moderator* even published his obituary, assuring its readers that Stephens had been an inoffensive young man and 'an excellent son and brother'.

Stephens escaped to France, disguised as a servant. It was then, at the age of twenty-three, that the former engineering student made a decision: he would break the power of the British Empire. Where Young Ireland had failed, he would succeed. At that time, the empire he challenged was the greatest amalgam of territory and the mightiest economic and military power in the history of the world. It far exceeded the empires of Rome and Egypt, the Greeks and the Mongols in all their pomp. It controlled a quarter of the world's population and was master of sub-continents and great swathes of territory in every region and zone on earth. Yet Stephens set himself the task of stunting its inexorable progress and rolling it back from the place of its inception, its first colony. He never allowed any setback, disappointment or reversal to deflect him from his goal. He bore poverty, imprisonment, betrayal, rejection by his comrades, accusations of treachery and even military defeat with the stoical resignation of the first Christian martyrs. His confidence in his ultimate triumph was, from the outset, unassailable.

Energising him through all his trials was a version of Ireland's history which he summarised in his Fenian proclamation of 1867 and which he had imbibed growing up in a Catholic, nationalist family. It was a source of inexhaustible sustenance for him and became a central tenet for all those who sought Ireland's independence by force of arms:

We have suffered centuries of outrage, enforced poverty, and bitter misery. Our rights and liberties have been trampled on by an alien aristocracy, who treated us as foes, usurped our lands, and drew away from our unfortunate country all material riches. The real owners of the soil were removed to make room for cattle, and driven across the ocean to seek the means of living, and the political rights denied to them at home, while our men of thought and action were condemned to loss of life and liberty. But we never lost the memory and hope of a national existence. We appealed in vain to the reason and sense of justice of the dominant powers.[2]

The significance of these beliefs for Stephens and other nationalists is impossible to exaggerate: what was at stake was not merely the freedom of the Irish nation but the survival of the Irish race. This was a theme to which Stephens returned again and again, first expressed in a speech he made in Brooklyn on 25 May 1866, when he was in New York to raise funds and galvanise support for an armed rising in Ireland. He stated this core Fenian tenet when he said, 'unless our country is liberated the Irish race will be absorbed in this country, in England and in many other places. We will lose our identity and eventually disappear from the face of the earth.'

Though the Fenian proclamation conceded that 'Our appeals to arms were always unsuccessful', Stephens and the men who rose against the British government in 1848 nevertheless asserted their right to fight for independence

---

2   See Appendix 4 for the whole proclamation.

and invoked solidarity with those who in earlier times had died in the effort, notably Wolfe Tone and the United Irishmen who took up arms for an independent Irish republic in 1798. In so doing they drew on a powerful tradition of political martyrdom.

Nor was it simply the experience of combat during the Young Ireland rising that was seminal for the fledgling revolutionary. The movement's propaganda, disseminated through John Mitchel's newspaper, the *United Irishman*, convinced him that without a nationalist conscience Ireland's distinctive culture would be lost. The 'men of no property', the embodiment of the nation's soul to whom Mitchel appealed, were to become as important to Stephens' thinking as the exaltation of violence, hatred of all things English and contempt for democratic politics also advocated by Young Ireland.

After Stephens fled to France, he eventually surfaced on Paris' Left Bank. He and John O'Mahony, a cross-eyed fellow revolutionary exile from Limerick, with long hair swept back from his high brow, shared a room in a Paris tenement. Stephens, wielding a stick of charcoal, scrawled sweeping diagrams on its plaster walls. These illustrated his plans for a revolutionary organisation that would smash British power in Ireland. When not eking out a living as a translator, he lectured and hectored the international community of socialist, communist and anarchist exiles who made Paris of the 1850s a university of subversion.

Their Paris experience confirmed Stephens' and

O'Mahony's conviction that Ireland would only achieve independence by force of arms. Fortunately for the prospects of his plans, Stephens had already concluded that he was a military genius and therefore fully equipped to lead such a rising. More realistically, however, both men agreed that if they were to succeed they must first build a new type of revolutionary organisation, financed and supported by the Irish in America. O'Mahony's task was to mobilise the Irish in exile, while Stephens was to return home to construct the organisation that would succeed where the rising of 1848 had failed.

Unlike any previous Irish nationalist organisation, the one Stephens sought to create would combine the power of the Irish diaspora – what Stephens called 'the new and greater Ireland' – with that of the most virulent nationalist elements at home, to create an irresistible force for Irish independence. In order to build such an organisation he set himself the task of personally making contact with all the country's advanced nationalist elements. To do this he walked, he later boasted, 3,000 miles. He chose, however, an inauspicious time.

In 1856, as James Stephens tramped the roads of Ireland, the whole country was one great ossuary. The Famine had hacked such a great swathe of death through the country that many were interred in burial mounds, unmarked graves and even on beaches. Visitors remarked on the deserted hamlets and abandoned settlements. On his long march across the south and west of Ireland, much of it on roads built as part of famine relief schemes, Stephens passed countless houses with their thatch decaying, rooks roosting in chimneys and nettles around the doorstep. In the west, rain and sun had bleached the stones that peeped like exposed skeletons from under sheets of moss.

But even more evident than the empty fields was the shame. None spoke of what had happened. Visitors found that if in a moment of forgetfulness a blacksmith, pointing out a house that was a landmark, mentioned a family who no longer lived there, or an innkeeper spoke of a townland now deserted, they at once averted their eyes and tried to bite back their words.

Though forewarned that national consciousness was at a depressingly low ebb, Stephens never doubted his ability to resurrect the spirit that had fired the United Irishmen, Robert Emmet and Young Ireland. In Marta Ramón's biography *A Provisional Dictator* he is quoted as saying that 'the cause is not dead, but sleeping'. Yet he did not delude himself about the magnitude of the task confronting him, adding, 'Ireland lives and glows – but lives and glows in a trance.'

As he walked from town to town many must have taken Stephens for an actor in a melodrama, separated from his company. Leaning into the wind, his Penna Dutch hat casting a shadow over his watchful eyes and peevish mouth and his great cloak billowing in his wake, he strode with his head at a characteristically arrogant tilt.

Though he was a wanted man and every encounter

carried the risk of betrayal, his stride never faltered. Like a medieval pilgrim or a mendicant preacher, his fervour powered his limbs and quickened his heart. He was a good judge of men and never doubted his instinct. He knew that government spies were everywhere and that a single word about arms or risings, conspiracies or plots, secret societies or drilling was enough to condemn him to imprisonment or exile.

This was Stephens at his best – inspiring, inexhaustible, meticulous, self-sacrificing and with an instinctive organisational genius. He was immensely and, for once, justifiably proud of the group he created, but like a doting father he was loath to do anything that might endanger his offspring. He was equally protective of his personal esteem; both his greatest strength and fatal flaw was his very high opinion of himself. In any discussion the sole opinion that mattered was his; the sole insightful observation was his; the sole genuine concern was his. Stephens would look vaguely beyond the person speaking and then when he had finished – often before he had finished – would make his point, which was frequently unconnected with anything that had been said.

Yet for all his personal foibles, the organisation that Stephens established flourished during the 1860s and spread through the trade unions, the big Dublin drapery stores and the building, shoe-making and tailoring trades in the capital and the other Irish cities. Equally important, it proved exceptionally attractive to the Irish in exile on both sides of the Atlantic.

The particular brand of revolutionary nationalism that Stephens dispensed intoxicated many sections of the Irish population and made it the obvious inheritor of Ireland's political legacy. In Stephens' own day it enthralled many of the Young Ireland rebels who, from prison cells, penal colonies and American exile, continued to embody an adamantine hatred of British rule in Ireland. With its emphasis on the role of the dispossessed in achieving independence it was attractive to all those who regarded themselves as victims of British rule: the landless, the exiled, those living in Irish towns and cities making a living in precarious employment. Democracy was not part of the experience of these groups; justice was a tool of British tyranny and violence the only means of striking against the oppressor. There was nothing in what Stephens proposed that seemed exotic or alien to the Irish. They were the product of a violent world. Eviction for a tenant farmer often meant destitution or death for him and his family. Throughout Europe nationalists struggling for independence assumed that they would not succeed without recourse to violence: Stephens was no different.

In the early stages of planning and building, Stephens kept in touch with O'Mahony through a number of emissaries. Finally, in the spring of 1858, O'Mahony asked him, on behalf of nationalists in America, to establish a revolutionary organisation in Ireland. Insisting on the titles 'Chief Executive' and 'Provisional Dictator', Stephens swore in the first members in Peter Lagan's timber yard in Dublin's Lombard Street on 17 March. Sometimes referred to as the Irish Republican Brotherhood (IRB), but generally known as the Fenians – the name applied originally to the American branch – it was an oath-bound revolutionary organisation sworn to the establishment of an independent Irish republic by force of arms.

It is testimony to the impact of Stephens' movement that by 1864 the word 'Fenian' had acquired the associations with which it still resonates today, and already conjured up the image of a 'terrorist' armed with gun and bomb, bent on political assassination and the destruction of the established order.

From the outset, Stephens realised that the authorities' ability to infiltrate nationalist conspiracies, especially that of Wolfe Tone's United Irishmen in 1798, was a major reason for the failure of previous risings. The need to counter this, together with what Stephens had learned of continental revolutionary organisations while in Paris, shaped the structure of the IRB. Stephens was much influenced by the organisation of secret revolutionary societies which he came into contact with in continental Europe. His concern for secrecy was obsessive and remarked on by all who knew him. He carried this to such lengths that he even refused to give the movement a name, referring to it only as 'the organisation'. Its entire structure was designed to prevent penetration by the authorities. In theory each member knew the identity of no members other than his immediate associates. Michael Davitt, the founder of the

Land League and an active Fenian, complained that the organisation was morbidly preoccupied with secrecy and that this was one of the things which prevented it from gaining wider support.

Another influence was the Irish tradition of secret agrarian societies of the eighteenth and early nineteenth centuries, such as the Ribbonmen. Though these groups were chiefly concerned with settling grievances arising from their members' position as tenant farmers and land-less labourers, they adopted the rhetoric of national inde-pendence and viewed most of their hardships as the result of British rule.

The Fenians were divided into a number of 'circles', each comprising 820 men, under the command of an 'A' or a 'centre'. Each centre was responsible for nine sub-centres, each under a captain also known as a sub-centre. In turn, each of the captains had charge of nine sergeants, each of whom controlled nine privates. In theory, no man knew the identity of any member outside his own section, thereby preventing damaging penetration by agents of the British government.

The men who joined the organisation were, Stephens was convinced, the keepers of the flame of Irish nationalism. The landless labourers and the small tenant farmers, the unskilled workers in the towns, the craftsmen, clerks and shop assistants still cherished hopes of an independent Ireland, free from the oppression of British rule. It suited the Fenian leadership that many followers came to believe that Irish independence would be accompanied by a redistribution of land and that returning exiles would once more take possession of what was rightfully theirs.

Yet, though Fenian talk of a redistribution of wealth alarmed the respectable classes and thrilled supporters, it had very little influence on their actions. First and last Stephens and his followers were nationalists, and he often spoke of the need to let nothing distract them from the goal of Irish independence. However, he did nothing to deter his followers from assuming that Irish independence would somehow solve their economic and status concerns.

Nor did Stephens want democratic diversions to distract the movement from revolutionary action. In this he was helped by the collapse in the late 1850s of the Tenant Right League, an organisation created to improve the legal position of tenant farmers and a precursor of the much more important Land League. It sought to develop a parliamentary adjunct, led by John Sadleir and William Keogh. Once in parliament, however, Sadleir and Keogh devoted their energies to personal advancement with a degree of cynicism seldom exceeded. For many nationalists this dalliance with constitutional politics proved a grave disappointment and convinced them that they would achieve their goals only through more robust methods. When Stephens dismissed democratic politicians as 'corrupt, self-serving, demoralising and ineffective', his words resonated with those who had put their trust in Sadleir and Keogh.

To others, however, Fenian ideas were anathema. Among the movement's most resolute opponents was the formidable Archbishop of Dublin, Paul Cullen, who was convinced that the interests of the church lay in working with the established authorities to secure the position of the Catholic faith in Irish life. A consistent opponent of nationalist causes – which he associated with the threat of liberal ideas – he spoke against Young Ireland and the Tenant Right League. In his view, Fenianism was contaminated by the subversive ideology which characterised the oath-bound secret societies of which he had had such appalling experiences in Rome in 1848, when radicals had murdered the prime minister and driven Pope Pius IX from the Vatican.

There were, however, other prominent churchmen, notably Archbishop John McHale of Tuam, and many modest curates and obscure parish priests who had a favourable, or at least ambivalent, attitude to the movement. The tradition of strong clerical support for the national cause was embodied in the lives of Fr John Murphy, Fr Michael Murphy and Fr Philip Roche – heroes and legendary rebels of 1798. Nevertheless, John Devoy, acclaimed by Patrick Pearse – leader of the 1916 Easter Rising – as the greatest Fenian, was convinced that the opposition of Cullen and other leading church figures was a major reason why Fenianism ultimately failed.

Cullen's opposition, however, was insufficient to deny Stephens a major triumph in 1861, when Terence Bellew

McManus died in San Francisco. One of the Young Ireland rebels of the 1848 rising, McManus had been transported to Van Diemen's Land, from where he had escaped and made his way to America. When he died, Stephens saw that the movement of the old rebel's body, across America and then from Cork to Dublin's Glasnevin Cemetery, provided a unique opportunity to channel nationalist and religious sentiments into a great display of patriotic fervour.

Beyond all expectations, the funeral was a political success. Episcopal opposition meant that McManus' body lay in state not in a church but in the Mechanics' Institute. Nevertheless, thousands filed past to pay their respects as much to the cause for which he fought as to his personal qualities. Countless thousands watched a torchlight procession, seven miles long, snake its way like a river of fire through the darkened city.

The medium-term effect of this event was a great upsurge in recruitment for the movement. What's more, it cemented the union between the Irish and the American branches of Fenianism.

Yet conflict between Stephens and his associates across the Atlantic soon arose. Its cause, in Stephens' view, was the failure of the Fenians in America to focus exclusively on their allotted task. In his opinion O'Mahony was simply required to provide men, arms and money for the Brotherhood which Stephens would employ as he saw fit. As O'Mahony later complained, Stephens envisaged the role of the American branch in strictly limited terms as 'a money funder, not a directing mind'.

Meanwhile O'Mahony had constructed a powerful movement in America with headquarters in New York. From 1863 he convened conventions in major cities such as Chicago, Pittsburgh and Philadelphia. He opened shops for the sale of bonds issued by the Irish Republic, redeemable against its future government. At the height of its power in the 1860s O'Mahony claimed 30,000 activists.

Yet, Stephens was not satisfied: the meagre financial support from America was not enough to arm the vast numbers of men he claimed were drilling by night in secluded spots all over Ireland. It was largely to fill this funding gap that in 1863 he launched a newspaper, the *Irish People*, from an office in Parliament Street, appropriately near Dublin Castle, the seat of British power in Ireland. Stephens threw himself into the enterprise with characteristic élan. Its message barely within the boundaries of legality, the paper provided a heady cocktail of altruistic nationalism, glorification of patriotic martyrs and constant reminders of the influence and power of Fenianism in America. It proved an effective propaganda vehicle and was particularly influential among the Irish in England and Scotland.

The men who produced the newspaper were all central figures in the movement. Thomas Clarke Luby, a member of the editorial team, played a part in the foundation of the Brotherhood and with John O'Leary, the editor, had fought in the 1848 rising. Edward Duffy and Hugh Francis Brophy – when not recruiting and training Fenians – were responsible for distribution. Charles Kickham, virtually deaf and blind, was another veteran of 1848 who wrote for the paper, while the flamboyant Jeremiah O'Donovan Rossa was its manager. Later, as a prisoner, O'Donovan Rossa came to personify the suffering of those who fought for Irish independence, and was to become even greater in death when, in 1915, Patrick Pearse delivered his most famous oration over his grave, the grave of 'our Fenian dead'. In life, O'Donovan Rossa was a gifted propagandist with a vitriolic tongue and a keen eye for an enemy's weakness. Almost unnoticed in the *Irish People*'s print room was a man who folded the papers as they flopped from the presses: Pierce Nagle, a native of Tipperary, was a former teacher whose role in subsequent events was to prove crucial.

Meanwhile, in 1861, the cataclysm of the Civil War engulfed America. Inevitably – and in some cases with alacrity – many Irish-Americans were caught up in a brutal and destructive conflict that prefigured the carnage of the Great War. About 150,000 Irishmen fought for the Union and 40,000 for the Confederacy. There were even several Irish regiments, the most famous of which, the Corcoran Legion, included many men like John O'Mahony who saw the Civil War as a preamble to and preparation for a conflict across the water.

On this side of the Atlantic Stephens was seeking to exploit the strong Irish presence in the British army. John

O'Leary undertook to spread Fenianism among the British forces, encouraged by the knowledge that of the 26,000 British troops stationed in Ireland in 1865, about half were Irish. Stephens boasted that 8,000 of them had taken the Fenian oath. He also claimed to have made major inroads among the 600,000 Irish immigrants and their children living in Britain. There is no doubt that exiles and their first-generation children found Fenianism extremely attractive.

In April 1865, Colonel Thomas J. Kelly arrived in Ireland as O'Mahony's personal envoy. His task was to report back on the feasibility of a rising. He was the first of many veteran officers of the Civil War to arrive that spring and their numbers increased because of the report he sent back to America: there was good reason to hope for a successful rising. Kelly became the secretary to the committee Stephens set up in Dublin to plan the rising.

As 1865 opened, developments boded well for the long awaited rising. In January Stephens claimed to have 85,000 trained men, eager for action and wanting only weapons. During the summer, Fenians demobbed from both Union and Confederate armies made their way to Ireland. The build-up of arms was proceeding apace and though Stephens griped relentlessly about the inadequacy of American funds, the circulation of the *Irish People* continued to rise.

Additionally, the anticipation of the rank and file created an irresistible momentum: there was a feeling among the members that this was a once-in-a-generation opportunity to strike a decisive blow for Irish freedom. Everything suggested imminent action. Then the authorities swooped.

On the evening of 14 September 1865, police descended on the office of the *Irish People* while simultaneously arresting key figures in Clonmel, Leeds, Sheffield, Salford and Manchester. The effectiveness of this operation suggests detailed knowledge of the inner workings of the organisation. In Cork, they discovered a list of British army Fenians, while in Fleetwood, Lancashire and Belfast they uncovered significant arms caches.

Stephens, meanwhile, holed up in Fairfield House in the sedate Dublin suburb of Sandymount, avoided capture for two months. On 11 November, however, while he was conferring with Kickham, Duffy and Brophy, a squad of uniformed police, led by detectives, sealed off the street and surrounded the house. They arrested all four leading Fenians and hauled them off to Richmond Gaol.

Brought before the court, Stephens, displaying his genius for self-dramatisation and grandiose gestures, refused to acknowledge its legitimacy, declaiming from the dock, 'I defy and despise any punishment it [British law] can impose on me.' His followers expected nothing less of him.

What followed is the stuff of boys' own adventure fiction and was proof, for many contemporary commentators, that in countering the Fenians the British authorities often displayed appalling incompetence. Stephens was housed at the heart of Richmond Gaol, in the hospital wing on the third floor. His cell was on a short corridor. At one end there was a locked door, guarded by two policemen. At the other, two doors: one timber and one iron, which could only be opened by a special pass key locked in the governor's office.

There were only three cells on this corridor: Kickham's and Stephens' separated by that of a jailbird, McLeod. The governor intended McLeod to act as an early warning device. He had a gong to raise the alarm at the sound of anything suspicious. The prison governor, Mr Marquess, was so confident in the security of the prison that he had no military guard. Four policemen were stationed inside the main entrance and others were dotted around the building. In the event of an emergency, support could be summoned from the nearby Portobello Barracks, where cavalry and artillery were stationed.

Thomas Kelly, who had provisionally taken command of the Fenians, devised a two-part plan to spirit away their chief. The first was to get Stephens to the prison's outer wall on the Circular Road. This part of the scheme depended on two prison workers, Daniel Byrne and John Breslin. Byrne was a night watchman at the prison and though he had aroused the suspicion of the authorities on a number of occasions, remarkably he remained in his post. Breslin, however, was the key man. His job was to accompany the prison doctor on his rounds and then revisit the cells to administer the prescribed medicines. Consequently, he had the run of the prison and was ideally placed to maintain contact between Stephens and those planning his escape.

Kelly inducted both John and his brother Michael Breslin into the movement. Michael was a clerk in the office of the police superintendent and he became the link between Kelly and the prison, as he was able to go there in his police uniform without arousing suspicion.

John Breslin got into the governor's office and made an impression of the key to the steel door on Stephens' corridor. As part of his job, he already had access to the cell key. All he had to do was plan a safe route to the outside wall. The one chosen involved a number of hazards. Stephens was to be led to the stairs and down to the ground floor. Breslin would use his key to open the door to the exercise yard. All that stood between the yard and the outside wall was the governor's garden, surrounded by a high wall. Breslin estimated that the ladder used to light the gas lamps in the yard would reach the top of this wall.

Once Stephens reached the outside wall the second part of Kelly's plan would come into effect. On the other side of the Circular Road a body of armed Fenians would be waiting for Stephens' signal. Their job was to act as a bodyguard and clear an escape route for their leader. A handful of gravel thrown over the wall would signal that he had arrived at the agreed spot. When the time was right, John Ryan, an IRB organiser and a key figure in the rescue, would imitate the quacking of a duck as a sign to his comrades to spring into action. Everything was in place for one o'clock on the morning of 24 November 1865.

The weather was perfect. It was a dark, overcast night and the steady rain kept the patrolling peelers under shelter. But as the bodyguard met at Lynch's public house in Camden Street, near the prison, things started to go wrong.

John Devoy had picked a dozen stalwart men who were competent in the use of arms. They were promised revolvers, but none had arrived and they were disgruntled. At the last minute, Devoy and Ryan had to scurry about the city to gather arms. By midnight, all but four of the men were armed.

They took up their positions around the prison. They checked the rope they'd earlier concealed and settled down for a long wait. Immediately, however, they heard a duck quacking. The men looked at Ryan in bemusement. He went off to investigate.

'There are ducks in that garden opposite the prison,' he explained incredulously.

Inside the prison, there were also problems. As Breslin unlocked the steel door and then Stephens' cell, they heard McLeod stirring. The two men held their breath but the convict made no further noise.

They reached the wall between the exercise yard and the governor's garden. It now became evident that the ladder was far too short to reach the top of the wall. Breslin bundled Stephens into a sentry box and returned to the prison to get the watchman, Daniel Byrne. Together they went to the dining-room and unlocked the doors. Breslin and Byrne then carried two large dining-tables to the base of the wall. One was set on top of the other and the ladder placed on them. Stephens scrambled to the top of the eighteen-foot wall. But no provision had been made for him to get down into the governor's garden.

As Stephens gazed down from the top of the wall, he made out, immediately below him, the roof of a tool shed. He had no option but to risk sliding onto the shed, hoping the noise would not alert the warders. It worked. He reached the outer wall and hid in the shade of the pear tree at its base. The stones swished onto the pavement of the Circular Road. He waited for endless minutes. Then he heard the slap of a rope against the inside of the wall. He scrambled up, his hands greasy with rain and sweat. From the top of the outer wall, the drop was terrifying. This time there was no garden shed to break his fall.

'Fasten the rope to the top of the wall,' Devoy hissed. 'Quick!'

'There's nothing to tie it to!' came the hoarse reply as Stephens teetered on the rim of the wall. The men below formed a circle, making a net of their linked arms.

'Jump!' Devoy ordered. 'Jump!'

By the time Daniel Byrne raised the alarm, Stephens was warming himself in front of Mrs Boland's fire in Brown Street. The elderly lady provided one of the many safe houses available to Fenians on the run. Stephens was never recaptured and shortly afterwards he slipped out of the country.

His co-conspirators, however, were not so fortunate. John O'Leary and Thomas Luby, arrested in the raid on the *Irish People* offices, were sentenced to twenty years' penal servitude and Charles Kickham to fourteen. The most severe punishment, however, was reserved for O'Donovan Rossa. In 1858, the authorities had arrested and imprisoned him, holding him without trial for seven months. In July 1859 they released him on condition that he stayed out of trouble. When in 1865 he again appeared before the court charged with high treason he expected the worst, and the manner in which he defended himself seemed calculated to ensure that he suffered the full wrath of British judicial might.

His defence was a model of O'Donovan Rossa's style. According to B. Jenkins' *The Fenian Problem*:

> He cross-examined the informers in fierce fashion, he badgered the detectives, he questioned the police, he debated with the crown lawyers, he argued with the judges, he fought with the crown side all round.

Having antagonised everyone on whom his fate depended, he ensured that the judge, Mr Justice Keogh, had every reason to detest him: he insisted on his right to read aloud all the pieces from the *Irish People* cited in evidence against him. This he did, hour after hour after hour, particularly relishing those pieces in which the judge himself was the object of odium, described as Britain's lackey and a traitor to his nation. For good measure, he denounced the trial as a farce – accusing the government of seizing papers vital to his defence, packing the jury with men hostile to nationalism and appointing Keogh – whom he likened to Norbury, infamous for his savage treatment of the United Irishmen – to conduct the trial.

Unsurprisingly, perhaps, Keogh condemned O'Donovan Rossa to penal servitude for life.

Meanwhile, though Stephens was free and glorying in the propaganda value of his rescue, his days as the moving force in the movement were running out. His escape increased the impetus for an immediate rising just as the British authorities intensified their campaign against the Fenians. In the final weeks of 1865, the government round-up gathered pace. There was no let-up with the turn of the year: the authorities suspended habeas corpus – thereby allowing arrest and imprisonment without trial – and the subsequent trawl of the Dublin area led to the internment of almost 200 leading Fenians. Influential elements in the organisation blamed Stephens for missing the opportunity presented by the uniquely propitious combination of circumstances that existed in 1865. Their misgivings were confirmed when, shortly after his escape, he again postponed the rising until 1866.

Whether the chill of his Richmond cell had cooled Stephens' ardour or whether he simply felt the situation in America made the outcome too doubtful is uncertain. Certainly, American developments were not promising. For just as the operation of the home movement had been compromised by Pierce Nagle, who had been informing from inside the *Irish People* press office since March 1864, that in America was similarly undermined by James McDermott, an Irish-American in whom John O'Mahony, despite many warnings, retained total confidence. Not only had McDermott been working for the British secret service for many years, he also had a genius for fomenting rancour among the Fenian leaders.

Exploiting the resentment of those Fenians who were growing impatient with O'Mahony's and Stephens' caution, McDermott spurred on those who believed the first blow for Irish freedom should be struck not in Ireland but in Canada. The chief advocate of this Canadian strategy was the vice-president of the New York militia, Colonel William Randall Roberts, who like so many leading Fenians was a battle-hardened veteran of the Civil War. Roberts was shrewd and ambitious, with a languid manner and a cynical eye. He regarded the wariness of O'Mahony and Stephens as congenital. The way forward, he believed, lay in exploiting the Anglo-American rift by grabbing a base in Canada. Roberts was convinced this would instantly transform the standing of the Irish Republic 'almost established'. He claimed that he had received a personal assurance from President Andrew Johnson that the USA would 'recognise the accomplished facts', that is, if the Fenians established a base in Canada, the American government would deem the government there 'the Irish Republic in exile'.

At the time this scheme, which today smacks of fantasy,

appeared far more realistic. Relations between the USA and Britain were poor. The American president and his secretary of war, Edwin M. Stanton, bitterly resented Britain breaking the blockade of the Southern states and sinking Union ships during the Civil War. They were prepared not only to make available to the Fenians surplus army supplies, weapons and ships, but also to turn a blind eye to their military activities. What's more there were reasonable grounds for hoping for help from both Irish- and French-Canadians. The latter were generally hostile to British rule and specifically to the proposal to unite the provinces into a single British Dominion of Canada.

Stephens deplored Roberts' scheme and expressed his disgust with characteristic vigour. What he saw as the Canadian diversion was unacceptable not only because Roberts was usurping his authority to dictate policy, but also because it diverted men and resources from the Irish theatre. To reassert his authority and raise money for activities in Ireland, Stephens went to America where he again pledged himself to a rising: 1866 was now to be 'the year of action'. But the response was poor. Consequently, pleading that he had only 4,000 rifles in the whole of Ireland, he begged another deferment.

But the tide in favour of action was now irresistible, and Stephens, in the words of John Mitchel, was like a man try-ing to hold back wolves by the ears. This tide finally swept him away and the Fenian inner circle ousted Stephens and put Kelly in charge of implementing immediate military action. However, it was not until a meeting in New York on 15 December 1866 that Stephens was formally deposed. Tempers became so inflamed that Captain John Mc-Cafferty would have shot Stephens if Kelly had not stood between the two men. There were other threats, however, which Kelly could not deflect.

The British authorities were convinced that a rising was imminent and acted accordingly. In the early months of 1866 they arrested 3,000 suspected Fenians and purged the army, with 150 men brought before a court martial. Many Fenians were flogged before their regiment, others transported, and suspect units were transferred to outposts of the Empire.

In April 1866, stung by charges of cowardice and anxious to pre-empt Roberts, O'Mahony sanctioned an attack on Campobella, an island off the Canadian mainland. British gunboats appeared in the area and effectively scuppered the plan.

In May 1866 Roberts launched a second Canadian adventure when a Fenian force crossed the Niagara river unopposed, occupied the undefended Fort Erie and settled down to wait for reinforcements which did not material-ise. Having repelled an attack by Canadian militia, they soon ran out of food and drifted away in small, despondent clusters.

These events signalled a significant change in the nature of the movement. Stephens, ever conscious of anything that might undermine his absolute authority, had grasped this before many others. Fenianism was no longer a monolithic organisation with the American branch a mere 'money funder' for a home organisation controlled by Stephens. Not only was the American branch fragmented, it was now seeking to direct policy.

Kelly's appointment signalled another important change: the tenor and nature of his leadership was entirely new. Kelly and his associates were men of the sort produced by many wars, and violence was the natural expression of their political aims. Inured to death, schooled in rigid discipline, their principles were loyalty, courage, self-sacrifice and camaraderie in the cause of national independence. They were idealists of the most dangerous kind. The American Civil War had given them the chance to take responsibility for their own lives while exercising authority over men. It bestowed respect and self-belief. It reinforced their national identity while exposure to the republican culture of the USA quickened their nationalist aspirations. Now, the Civil War over, the Fenian cause provided an ample opportunity to use their skills in pursuit of their personal and political ambitions.

In January 1867, Kelly crossed the Atlantic to begin plans for a rising. One of those who accompanied him was Michael O'Brien, who had worked with Stephens to make the McManus funeral such a success. The rising they envisaged was in effect a guerrilla war waged against British rule and its agents. It was designed to disrupt communications, attack police barracks and harass the government at every opportunity. At some stage, they expected reinforcements of arms and men from America.

The first stage, planned for February 1867, was an attack on the arsenal at Chester Castle. Said to hold 30,000 stands of arms, its capture would at a stroke supply the movement with all the munitions it needed. The scheme involved seizing a train to take the weapons to Holyhead, where they would be transported to Ireland by a commandeered mail boat.

Once more an informer scuppered the plan: John Joseph Corydon kept the authorities apprised of developments. Corydon's defection was a serious blow on several levels. Not only was he a centre, with direct control of over 800 Fenians and in frequent contact with all the organisation's leading figures, but for most of 1865 and 1866 he was a courier between Ireland and the USA.

Based on the information Corydon provided, the authorities strengthened the castle guard and called out local volunteers. When, on the appointed day, Irishmen from all over Britain, including many from Manchester and Liverpool, started to converge on Chester, not only was a detachment of the 54th Regiment at hand, but the morning papers reported the Fenian plan.

Once more, the plot collapsed in disarray, with demoralised Fenians throwing incriminating munitions from the trains taking them home from Chester. Others did not escape so easily, especially those who tried to get back to Ireland on the Holyhead ferry. Detectives from

G Division – which dealt with counter-subversion – of the Dublin Metropolitan Police met them as they walked down the gangplank. Among these was John Flood, head centre for England. Another was Francis McAuliffe, a fantasist and self-publicist who travelled around the country delivering public lectures on Ireland's misfortunes. He described himself in the publicity for these as 'a Knight of the Holy Roman Empire, a former commander of the Federal American forces and of the Papal Brigade'. There is no evidence to support his claim to any of these titles or experiences. McAuliffe hovered on the periphery of Fenian politics, basking in reflected glory and claiming to have the ear of those who shaped policy. Active Fenians regarded him as an idiot.

Meanwhile, Kelly, the man who was in reality the moving force in Fenianism, affirmed his commitment to a rising in Ireland. As an experienced soldier, Kelly, like Irish revolutionaries before and since, realised that he could not achieve the military overthrow of British power in Ireland. At best he hoped his men would give a good account of themselves and reaffirm the tradition of armed struggle. The rising, set for 5 March, was to be largely symbolic, a means of maintaining the morale and momentum of the movement.

General Gustave Cluseret, a French mercenary and supporter of nationalist causes, and his Italian subordinate, General Fariola, had charge of the fighting in Ireland. The Fenian leaders had recruited them because of their sympathy with Fenianism and their Italian experience of military action in a nationalist cause. Central to the rising, however, was Patrick Massey, whose task it was to capture Limerick Junction.

Cluseret believed that there was not 'a chance in 2,000 of the rising succeeding'. Though he claimed that 'personal grievances' weakened the movement, he was greatly impressed by the centres, who were 'noble and self-sacrificing'. Their tenacity proved capable of enduring almost any disappointment and overcoming any setback. To this extent, as Ramón says in *A Provisional Dictator*, the movement Stephens had built reflected his greatest quality.

As before, the rising was condemned to failure before it began. The authorities, courtesy of the insidious Corydon, were forewarned. They arrested Massey as his foot touched the platform at Limerick Junction. Faced with sharing O'Donovan Rossa's fate, Massey told the British the little they didn't already know. On hearing of Massey's capture, Cluseret fled. Effectively leaderless, uncoordinated and without any liaison with the Americans, the rising went off at half-cock.

The rising of 1867 consisted of a series of isolated, uncoordinated skirmishes in which many individuals fought with courage and skill without achieving any significant success. In Rathmines and Drogheda, Cork, Limerick and Tipperary, Fenian forces confronted armed police and soldiers, and there were minor incidents in Clare, Queen's County (Laois) and Louth. Cut telegraph lines, a smouldering barracks in Burnfort, ten killed and fifty wounded – this was the total of events. There was no rising in Ulster. The authorities effectively employed flying columns to disperse the rebels and later mop them up.

One of those who did distinguish himself was Timothy Deasy, a Civil War veteran and a leading figure in the movement who was to play a significant role in events in Manchester later in the year. During the rising he commanded troops in Millstreet. Michael O'Brien – another Irish veteran of the Civil War who had worked with Stephens on the organisation of Terence Bellew McManus' funeral – achieved one of the few successes of 1867. He led 2,000 Cork men in the capture of the police barracks at Ballyknockan, County Wicklow, and went on to sabotage the Great Southern and Western Railway, derailing the Dublin express. Another success – the capture of the coastguard station and its weapons at Knockadoon, County Cork – was not followed up and the advantage was soon dissipated.

As if to mock the failed rebels, soon after the British had put down the rising, on 20 May, *Erin's Hope* appeared off the coast of Donegal, laden with 8,000 rifles and forty Fenian officers, veterans of the Civil War. Before it returned to New York with its cargo, it dropped a number of men into the sea off Sligo's Strada Point. When they emerged gasping from the chill water the local police were waiting to arrest them.

In the mopping-up operation that followed, soldiers

Timothy Deasy
Courtesy of Mercier
Archives

and police combed the hills where the Fenians had once trained. Subsequently, judges handed down long terms of penal servitude and three men, John McCafferty, Patrick Doran and Thomas F. Bourke, were sentenced to death. John McCafferty was the man who, but for Kelly's restraining hand, would have shot Stephens. While the convicted men stood under the shadow of the gallows, a fierce debate raged within the British political class. A powerful body of opinion clamoured for the men to be hanged, claiming that anything less would encourage further violent sedition and convince the rebels they could strike at the foundations of British rule without fear of incurring the ultimate punishment. But for the intervention of the US government on their behalf, the men – all veterans of the Civil War – might well have hanged. The government commuted McCafferty's and Doran's sentences. However, as the day of the execution approached Bourke prepared for death. It was only after a deputation of MPs crowded into the prime minister's London home that Lord Derby issued a reluctant reprieve. It was a decision his enemies later used against him, claiming that only the utmost rigour of the law would break the Fenians.

Having affirmed its authority, however, the British government treated the vanquished with magnanimity. Whether this clemency was an act of rare statesmanship or proof of a lack of government resolve, critics of the government were right about one thing: neither the failure of the rising of 1867 nor the treatment of those who took part had broken the Fenians or deflected them from their course. Nor had it reduced the sympathy of the Irish people for the Fenian cause. Pro-rebel demonstrations took place in Cork and elsewhere throughout Munster. A crowd of 8,000 attacked the police as they were taking the men from *Erin's Hope* to gaol, killing one peeler and wounding forty.

And, as the events which took place in Manchester during the final months of 1867 demonstrate, those who feared that the tentacles of the Fenian conspiracy reached into every British city that was home to the Irish were about to have those fears confirmed.

2

MANCHESTER: HOME FROM HOME

Tears ran down the old man's grime-encrusted face. He stood on the hospital steps and turning to the crowd, held the tiny, headless corpse above his head. Men roared, children screamed, women wailed. The old man staggered backwards towards Fr Hearne. The priest took the child, cradled him in the crook of his left arm and raising his right hand, silenced the crowd.

Cholera killed little John Brogan. But the medical student who decapitated the child for research purposes awoke a deep-rooted fear in the Manchester Irish. The near riot that erupted in 1832 when doctors returned the child's body to his grandfather in a sealed coffin was an indication of the engrained fear that the Manchester Irish had of the authority's hostility towards them: what was merely an act of appalling insensitivity was interpreted as the murder or mutilation of an innocent child because he was Irish.

The promise of work and the city's proximity to their homeland attracted the Irish to Manchester. In 1851, thirteen per cent of the population of Manchester and Salford was Irish born. Liverpool apart, there was no city in England more Irish. Those who arrived in the 1847–1851 period were victims of the Famine and destitute. To feed them an additional poor rate burden fell on resentful householders. Popular mythology had it that the Irish were prepared to work for less than the going rate and thus depressed wages. Though typhus was already raging in the English cities before the Irish arrived, nevertheless, it became known as 'Irish fever'. In 1847 an outbreak of cholera decimated the slum population and reinforced the popular association of the Irish with poverty and death.

Nothing did more to fix the notion of the teeming Irish ghetto in the popular mind than Little Ireland, a low, swampy, poverty-stricken area of Manchester. J. P. Kay's 1832 pamphlet, *The Moral and Physical Condition of the Working Classes Employed in the Cotton Manufacture in Manchester*, catapulted it to notoriety: 'About 200 are crowded together in an extremely narrow space, and are chiefly the lowest Irish.'

Cellars, ceilings black with cockroaches, housed as many as could find space on the fetid straw covering the floor. When Engels visited in 1844, researching for his book *The Condition of the Working Class in England*, he found that 'A horde of ragged Irish swarm about here, as filthy as the swine that thrive upon the garbage heaps and in the puddles ... such a hateful and repulsive spectacle ... can hardly be equalled.'

A journalist who lifted the lid on the horrors was guaranteed avid readers. In 1899 Robert Blanchford went undercover for the *Sunday Chronicle* and plunged into:

> ... miles of narrow, murky streets ... involuted labyrinths of courts and passages and covered ways where a devilish ingenuity shuts out light and air. Everywhere there was filth, broken pavements, ill-set roads covered with rubbish, stagnant pools of water, and dark, narrow, dilapidated, built-in hovels.

His middle-class readers were appalled. Many accused him of exaggeration, if not blatant lies.

Blanchford was not reporting from darkest Africa or the bowels of a teeming oriental city. He was describing Manchester as it was after the slum clearance that swept away the worst of the Deansgate rookeries in the 1870s. The city where the seminal events of 1867 took place was certainly no better than these journalists found thirty years later.

Contemporary newspaper accounts captured the dread typically provoked by the alien Irish hordes, who came to embody all the problems of the burgeoning industrial cities – including crime and drink. They shaped the attitudes of the host community. Court records show that Irish immigrants committed a disproportionate number of minor offences, though not more serious crimes. The press invariably referred to the immigrants who appeared in court reports and accounts of disorder as 'low Irish' and never failed to inform readers that they were 'of no education' or 'of imperfect education'. The Irish saw the police as enemies and attacked any who ventured into Little Ireland. They had a reputation for resisting arrest, and would, in the words of one policeman, 'struggle until the shirt had been torn from their backs'.

Anti-Catholicism, endemic to every stratum of English society, fortified hostility to the Irish. The Ancoats area of the city was popularly known as 'Fenian Manchester'. More than anywhere else in Britain, Manchester epitomised all that was dangerous about the Irish. The events which unfolded in September 1867 made the city the centre of Fenian activity and the focus of the fears that gripped every tier of British society from the government downwards.

The first Irish to settle in Manchester made their homes in Newton, in the north-east of the city – later known as Irish Town and then Angel Meadow. Wherever the Irish settled they marked their territory by building a church and in 1829 they built St Patrick's on Livesey Street. Soon they spread to nearby Ancoats. The third place they colonised was Chorlton-on-Medlock, where they opened St Augustine's church in 1820 and in 1832 *The Manchester Guardian* first referred to the area as Little Ireland. It wasn't long before this obscure district of Manchester gained an international reputation and became a magnet for every social commentator of the day.

Cellar-dwellers formed the bottom stratum of urban society. The basements they lived in were let or sublet by the occupants of the houses above. Generally, the rent was half that for a house and consequently the poorest workers and those in irregular employment gravitated towards them. Many – though by no means all – were Irish and they were generally casual labourers, hawkers and street traders. Large numbers worked as porters in Manchester's Smithfield Market or as dealers in second-hand clothes. However, half the Ancoats Irish cellar-dwellers worked in the cotton mills.

Once an Irish family settled in Manchester they often became the focal point for further immigration – other family members and neighbours moving from Ireland to join them. They provided a welcoming smile, accommodation and help to find a job. Yet they never lost the sense that they were outcasts, and this created strong communal ties that bound them together. Nor was it only the native Mancunians who drove them together. There were those who, though strangers themselves, sought to subject the Manchester Irish to the oppression they had hoped to escape.

Orangemen had set up England's first County Grand Lodge in Manchester early in the nineteenth century. The country's first anti-Catholic riot of the nineteenth century, directed at the Manchester Irish, followed in 1807 with subsequent attacks in 1830 and 1834 further heightening tension. Prejudice also afflicted the Irish in a less spectacular manner. It confined them to the worst jobs and kept them poor. The 1836 commission into the state of the Irish poor in Great Britain heard that they were 'prevented from advancing from feelings of jealousy. A manufacturer would prefer employing English to Irish simply on the grounds of they being Irish and not being worse workmen.'

As conditions in Ireland deteriorated, culminating in the Famine of 1847, the pressure to emigrate became irresistible. The influx of destitute, disease-ridden spectres during the 1840s heightened the hostility of the host community and confirmed its belief that the Irish were a threat. In the short term, they overwhelmed the city's poor relief provision.

Between 1841 and 1843 Manchester Poor Law Unions removed 2,647 Irish from the township because they had no right of settlement and therefore no right to relief. In 1847 the Unions reported that 1,500 Irish had arrived over a few weeks. This was at a time when droves of immigrants from surrounding Lancashire were also descending on the city. Of Manchester's population of 400,000 in 1851, fifty-five per cent were born elsewhere. Of these, 52,500 were Irish-born. This made the Irish by far the largest group of newcomers. In 1851 Lancashire had the highest proportion of Irish-born people of any British county, about thirteen per cent.

From the 1850s Manchester was an enclave of Irish political separatism, second only to London. It was one of the first British cities to establish Fenian circles. In addition to the settled Irish community there was a constant flow of 'harvestmen' who passed through every year on their way to Cheshire, Yorkshire, Lincolnshire and the east of England. By 1861 the Irish-born made up one in five of the city's population. They formed a cohesive and distinctive community. More than anything else their priests held the Irish together. Invariably Irish and Irish-speakers, like most of their parishioners, they were the exile's last link with home. They had much in common with their congregation and identified with them against English employers and authorities.

As the frequent complaints of English bishops testify, they were fiercely nationalistic and reinforced the obsession of their parishioners with Irish affairs. Fr Daniel Hearne, a renowned Irish Town priest, incensed by the deterioration of conditions in Ireland and the onset of the Famine, became progressively more radical in his politics. The ideas of the Young Irelanders captivated him and in expressing his support for them he aroused opposition from other clergy and even sections of his own congregation, eventually forcing him to withdraw from Irish Town and then Manchester and return to Ireland. He was typical of the Manchester clergy in Irish areas, as was evident, for instance, in the North-East Manchester by-election of 1891 when only one of the constituency's Catholic priests failed to campaign for the Home Rule candidate.

The church consolidated and extended the Irish

character of large areas of the city. St Patrick's, for instance, which served the Catholics of Angel Meadow, soon sprouted other institutions: a convent of the Presentation Order, St Patrick's Boys' School, St Bridget's Orphanage and, in 1845, a community of Christian Brothers. Yet, though the Irish were putting down roots, competition in the workplace between indigenous unskilled workers and the Irish remained intense.

This competition was most acute in the building trade where the Irish were in the forefront of trade union activity and conspicuously active in all the major building disputes in Manchester from 1833 to 1870. The records of the Manchester Bricklayers Labourers' Union confirm this. In 1856 it had 900 members, organised into nine lodges. All the officials were Irish, as were the great majority of members. The union was part of community life, for its trustee and treasurer was Canon Toole, parish priest of St Wilfred's, Hulme, an area with a sizeable Irish community. The Irish in Manchester had a strong tradition of cooperation and it was their shared religious faith which cemented their unity more than anything else. The majority of Irish Catholics were practising – they went to church every week. This marked them off from the rest of the working-class community.

What's more, the church in Manchester gloried in its Irishness. It commemorated the feast of St Patrick with Masses, with entertainment in the church hall, the Blessing of Shamrock and a Catholic rally held in the Free Trade Hall. In all this the parish school was an adjunct of the church. Until the Great War, virtually all Catholic children received their education in Catholic schools. And it was this combination of faith and national identity that made the city's reaction to the Irish so antipathetic.

Their hosts attributed many of the reputed faults of the Irish to their pernicious faith, to which they were believed to be uncritical adherents. However, this was not their only deficiency. The English also dismissed them as racially and intellectually inferior to the Anglo-Saxons and claimed they were totally incapable of governing themselves, representing, as they did, a lower form of civilisation. And there were many in the great conurbation who were ready to put up a fight against these pernicious invaders.

In the 1830s militant anti-Catholics formed the Salford Operative Protestant Society to spread their ideas among workers. The Manchester equivalent was the Protestant Tradesmen's and Operatives' Association. Both organisations were extremely voluble and the local press provided sympathetic coverage. Dr Giacento Achilli, a renegade Dominican friar and one of the first anti-Catholic rabble-rousers, was an avid proponent of these societies' efforts to impregnate popular culture with anti-popery. He often attracted large crowds, which he regaled with tales of virtuous Protestants rotting in papal dungeons.

Others ploughing the same furrow of bigotry in the 1850s were Signor Alessandro Garazzi, Rev. Count Wlodarski and Baron and Baroness de Camin, both of whom had the background and aura of third-rate music hall acts. Many of their meetings sparked violence and, in the 1850s, a number of anti-Catholic riots, notably in Stockport and Manchester in 1852 and nearby Wigan in 1859.

The ranks of the militant anti-Catholics contained a number of national figures. Thomas Hughes, author of *Tom Brown's Schooldays*, and Charles Kingsley, one of the most prolific Victorian writers, played a role in promoting anti-Catholicism nationally. The most voluble proponent of this sectarianism was the notorious William Murphy, prize asset of the Protestant Evangelical Mission and Electoral Union, whose anti-Catholic roadshow attracted national attention in 1867. Wherever he went he provoked street battles. When he went to Birmingham that year the efforts of 400 troops, 1,000 peelers and countless special constables were not enough to prevent violent clashes.

All this trickled down to the English poor, drove a wedge between them and the Irish and by the 1860s created a strong anti-Irish tradition in parts of Manchester and Salford. Many blamed the Irish for the cotton famine of the 1860s that plunged Lancashire into destitution, forcing hundreds of thousands of people onto poor relief.

Manchester was a Fenian stronghold with a large and sympathetic Irish population. But it was also home to deep-seated anti-Irish and anti-Catholic sentiments, which had a major impact on subsequent events.

***

It was Edward O'Meagher Condon who, after the failure of the rising of March 1867, proposed Manchester as the venue for a meeting of leading Fenians to enable the movement to regroup and rededicate itself to revolutionary action. Like so many other leading figures he was a veteran of the American Civil War. Shrewd and wry, with the mien of a successful businessman, he cast piercing looks at his fellow Fenians as he moved around the city in preparation for the meeting. His detached scrutiny made many wary of him and needled others. As he moved from Angel Meadow to Ancoats and then Chorlton-on-Medlock, whispering to the key men in the organisation, he was wary of any slight and never forgave those who offended him.

The ease with which men like Condon were able to move around the city led those involved in countering Fenian activity in Ireland to complain about the laxity of the English police, claiming that subversives in Manchester enjoyed a freedom of action unheard of in Ireland. The events of 1867 suggest that there was some truth in this. In the aftermath of the rising in Ireland hundreds of Fenians, many of them Irish-Americans, were in hiding or on the run. The Irish authorities' pursuit of the nationalists was relentless and they arrested and charged hundreds. But they did not succeed in destroying the movement or capturing its most important figures. Its leader, Thomas J. Kelly, despite government efforts in both Ireland and England, remained at liberty and was as ebullient as ever. A battle-hardened veteran of the American Civil War, Kelly's resolution, courage and irrepressible optimism aroused fierce loyalty among Fenians. Having trained for the priesthood, Kelly was now as fervent about saving Ireland's national soul as he had once been in saving sinners.

Though a realist and a man of action, Kelly shared the optimism of his predecessor, James Stephens. His aspirations, he believed, were more realistic than those of 'the chief', although like Stephens he had an unshakeable faith in his ability to break British power in Ireland. Stephens had created the means by which this could be done, but his indecision, his inability to grasp the opportunity for action and his addiction to intrigue and internal wrangling made him incapable of carrying it through. Action was Kelly's antidote to all problems – swift, forceful and audacious blows against Britain, delivered by experienced soldiers with tactical and leadership skills, would make Ireland ungovernable and force the British to accede to nationalist demands. Yet there were obstacles. Kelly believed the organisation in America had abandoned its original purpose and become no more than a debating society, and certainly not a fit instrument to direct a military campaign. What's more, funds from the USA had dried up.

Yet despite these concerns, the Manchester meeting was a triumph for Kelly. Held in September 1867, all its key figures were hewn from the same rock as the Fenian leader. Captain James Murphy, late of the 20th Massachusetts Infantry, and Colonel Ricard O'Sullivan Burke, the movement's chief procurement officer, chaired it. Because of intense government activity it proved impossible for many Fenians outside the area to attend but 150 delegates, having unanimously elected Kelly chief executive, enthusiastically endorsed his programme. As Kelly's fist, rising and falling like a steam hammer, drove home his points, a new stage in the Fenian struggle was born. The shy smile on Kelly's face betrayed his delight and exposed the gap in his teeth which was the result of a Confederate bullet that had shattered his jaw.

The meeting declared the home organisation independent of the American wing. Kelly now exercised the absolute control Stephens had always sought. Though a new American adjunct of the organisation, Clan na Gael, was created, it was clear from the outset that it was to have no policy role.

The convention also sanctioned expansion in those British industrial cities and towns with a significant Irish presence. Instead of returning home, the American officers were to attach themselves to areas of Fenian support and act as intermediaries between the executive and the local centre. In other ways the role of the Irish-American veterans was to become central: weekly membership dues were to provide funding which would enable them to stay in Europe in readiness for the next rising.

Condon, who was appointed Kelly's intermediary in Manchester, and had responsibility for the northern counties, from the Midlands to the Scottish borders, had already started to tighten up the organisation. Recent setbacks had punctured morale and many of Manchester's nine circles were low on numbers and virtually inactive. Condon consolidated committed members into three circles. Kelly, from his new headquarters in Manchester, directed a similar overhaul throughout the entire movement. James Murphy became head centre for Scotland and O'Sullivan Burke for the south of England. Timothy Deasy was to be stationed in Liverpool, another Fenian stronghold. Michael O'Brien, one of Ricard O'Sullivan Burke's comrades in the American Civil War, had worked with him in acquiring weapons. Now the convention gave him a roving commission as Kelly's factotum.

The most important decision, however, was to immediately begin planning for another armed rising. Kelly was ideally suited in both temperament and experience for this task. Bustling about the city from one meeting to another like a frantic entrepreneur anxious to clinch a deal, he was in many ways a typical Fenian. The man who was preparing to overthrow the established order was middle aged. As an adolescent growing up in Galway, his outlook was shaped by the trauma of the Famine. After a spell in a seminary convinced him that he didn't have a vocation to the priesthood he pursued another passion – newspapers. He served an apprenticeship as a printer and then followed many of his contemporaries in search of a better life in America. Immediately he threw himself into nationalist and labour politics within the Emmet Monument Association and the New York Printer's Union. The Emmet Society was a focus for fervent republican nationalists predisposed towards violence as the means of attaining their goals. The organisation reinforced Kelly's interest in revolutionary nationalism and introduced him to like-minded men. He joined the Fenians in 1858 as one of its early members. At this stage he demonstrated a staggering capacity for hard work and a relentless drive – expressed by the manner in which he stressed his point by hammering his clenched right fist into the palm of his left hand – which enthused his comrades and inspired them to feats of courage. Though firmly grounded in reality, he was innately optimistic: no matter how unpromising the situation, Kelly could always see a way through. All that was necessary was 'to keep up the steam'.

Together with 190,000 of his countrymen, Kelly fought in the Civil War, like most Irishmen, on the side of the Union. He distinguished himself with the 10th Ohio Regiment and rose to the rank of captain before he was severely wounded and invalided out in 1864. It took a skilful surgeon to remove the bullet from his jaw and disguise the hole it had punched in his chin. Kelly's goatee covered the scar but his tongue never lost the taste of the steel that had sliced through it.

He was convinced that his military service was a preparation for the fight for Irish freedom. Though he ran the newspaper he had founded, the *Nashville Democrat*, he had no hesitation in abandoning his business and taking ship for Ireland in preparation for the planned rising. He was one of the first officers to arrive and his task was to report to the American branch of the organisation on the readiness of the home organisation to take up arms.

It seems that his leadership was widely known among informed observers outside the movement, as in 1867 the *Liverpool Mercury* said of Kelly that 'he had more influence among the Brotherhood and stood higher in the confidence of his disaffected countrymen than even James Stephens, its founder'.

The Manchester meeting also confirmed the position of Captain Timothy Deasy. It is not entirely clear what Deasy's exclusive responsibilities were, though he was certainly Kelly's aide-de-camp and head of the organisation in Liverpool. Some claim he enjoyed the official title of Deputy Central Organiser of the Irish Republic and was responsible for liaison between Dublin and Manchester.

In many ways Deasy's life had run parallel to Kelly's. He was born in Clonakilty, County Cork, an area where the Famine cut great swathes through the population. His earliest memories were of the terror induced by starvation and disease, and he never lost the wide-eyed expression of someone who is amazed by all he sees; together with his smooth skin this gave him a child-like appearance. In 1847 he and his family sailed to America where, in 1861, he enlisted in the entirely Irish 9th Massachusetts Volunteer Infantry Regiment. Fighting in thirty-two engagements he showed conspicuous gallantry and leadership and though wounded in the battle of Spotsylvania, he remained in command of his company.

Deasy's war experience reinforced his nationalist fervour. It also left him with a total absence of fear. No one who had fought with him doubted his reckless courage. But he was also impetuous. While Stephens was cautious to the point of inactivity, Deasy was prone to rashness. By the end of the Civil War in 1865 he was an IRB captain and one of the first to arrive in Ireland in preparation for the rising. The Supreme Council immediately drafted him into the group planning the insurgency. It was then that he had his first encounter with the British authorities. While in the Fenian stronghold of Skibbereen, the police arrested him together with other Fenians. Unusually, they took their prisoners to England but, not for the last time, they failed to appreciate Deasy's importance and released him – on condition he left England and returned to America. Instead, he returned to Ireland and having spent some time in Belfast went to Dublin shortly after Stephens' arrest, and, with Kelly, played a leading role in the Fenian leader's escape from Richmond Gaol. He then accompanied Stephens first to France and then to the USA. As Kelly's representative, he participated in the invasion of Canada led by John O'Neill in June 1866. He then returned to Europe and played a central role in the events of 1867 when he took part in the Chester Castle raid and commanded men at Millstreet, County Cork, in the March rising. This time he evaded capture.

Deasy was Kelly's ideal second in command and the Fenian leader was delighted with his appointment. They shared the same formative experiences and inhabited the same mental world. They could sit in silence knowing exactly what the other was thinking.

Yet Kelly still had a major concern: he was anxious to ensure that his leadership was endorsed by the entire membership. Few Fenians from outside the area had been able to attend the Manchester meeting, so to enlist the support of the entire movement a further meeting was necessary. It was agreed that this would take place in Manchester some time in the autumn or early winter. In preparation for it Kelly, Deasy, Condon and other leading Fenians were constantly on the move, flitting in and out of the Irish areas of the city. The ebb and flow of Manchester's streets provided anonymity. They had a vibrant life of their own – with crowds drawn to the open markets at the weekend, the filling and disgorging of pubs, the warm chatter of audiences leaving the music halls and the shrieking of children at play on the streets. It was as hard to track an individual's movement as to spot a specific fish in a shoal of herring.

Yet the police knew something was afoot. Though the local peelers could not identify the leading Fenians, there were those who knew them all by sight and could pick them out, even on Manchester's bustling thoroughfares.

***

One day in September, as Condon walked along London Road, he spotted the informer John Joseph Corydon.

Condon stopped, bowed his head and looked from under the brim of his hat. Corydon was on the opposite pavement, walking towards him. The man's gait made Condon's heart thump. There was no mistake. Condon pushed his hand deeper into the recess of his overcoat pocket and squeezed the handle of his revolver.

Between two men who moved with the slow purposefulness of peelers, the rangy Corydon walked with his high-stepping gait, like a skittish foal. His copper hair and pale skin were as distinctive as his walk. Now they were directly across the road from him, only five or six strides away from Condon. He knew what he should do: cross the road, fall into step behind them. Then in a few minutes they would be in the throng of Piccadilly, bodies three deep at the kerb waiting to cross the road. He could then push right up against Corydon and ram the barrel against the back of his neck.

At that instant, a hansom cab passed along the road, obscuring his view. When it passed, he spotted his prey. But before he could cross the road, a brewer's dray blocked them out once more. He stepped forward, desperate to get to the other side before Corydon escaped. Then, running to the far kerb and raising himself on his toes, he scanned the swarm of heads. The city had swallowed them up.

Corydon was one of the most detested men in Ireland. Once one of Stephens' most valued lieutenants he had betrayed both the Chester raid and the rising of March 1867. Condon repeatedly reproached himself for missing his fleeting opportunity to kill the traitor and his premonition that he would live to regret his failure soon proved correct.

The police decision to bring Corydon to Manchester certainly boded ill. Condon knew there were warrants out for many of those involved in the March rising and the informer was certainly in the city to help police identify suspects. Corydon, despite his elevated status in the annals of infamy, was only one of the more notorious British spies to infiltrate the Fenian movement. What distinguished him from the merely venal was the extent of the damage he, as a long-standing informer occupying an extremely sensitive role in the organisation, was able to inflict. This was certainly partly because of his impeccable Fenian background.

Like many of those in the forefront of the organisation, Corydon was not born in Ireland. Observers both inside and outside the movement remarked on the powerful appeal of Fenianism to those born of Irish parents in Britain and America. Corydon was of Liverpool–Irish ancestry and emigrated to America, where he fought in the Civil War and later joined the Fenians. At about the same time he threw in his lot with the British authorities. His motives are unclear. At one time he claimed that he was not driven by greed but by contempt for his fellow conspirators.

Perhaps Corydon's low assessment of his comrades in conspiracy was justified. Kelly and Deasy would have argued that seven centuries of British rule had so sapped

Irishmen of self-respect that they despised their own and took themselves at the Englishman's estimation. However, the petty jealousies of the pricklish personalities in the Manchester organisation which surfaced in the days after Corydon arrived in the city perhaps help to explain the spy's jaundiced opinion.

Having let slip the opportunity to kill Corydon, Condon's immediate concern was to warn the membership of the traitor's arrival and tell them to stay off the streets and away from pubs and music halls. He walked to the homes of several trusted men and sent them to warn the centres and sub-centres.

William Melvin was sent to warn Thomas Bolger, a sub-centre in the city. When Melvin reached Bolger's home he found him deep in conversation with men he didn't know. It was impossible for him to pass on his message without alerting Bolger's guests that something was afoot, and not wanting to delay informing the others, he instead spoke to Bolger's brother, who lived next door.

When Bolger eventually received the message he was furious. Melvin's actions, he maintained, were a deliberate slight. He demanded that Kelly and Deasy hear his complaint and make a ruling. The resultant meeting took place on the evening of Wednesday 11 September. Once the matter was resolved to Bolger's satisfaction, the Fenian leaders made their way through the dark streets to the house of Henry Wilson, a second-hand clothes dealer whose business was based in his home. Like many in his trade, Wilson sometimes dealt in stolen goods. But that wasn't why the police were interested in him.

Wilson's was a safe house: Condon and Kelly had both stayed there when they first arrived in Manchester. The Fenians also used it as a postal address. That evening Kelly and Deasy went to Oak Street, abutting Smithfield Market, to check the post. By the time they got there the porters and hawkers, many of them Irishmen, had long gone to their beds in the huddled streets around the market. The gutters were clogged with cabbage leaves and oranges. And there was that smell, the all-pervading dampness of the city which seemed to ooze from the bricks of the ramshackle houses.

Wilson lived at the bottom of Oak Street. As they reached the top, the men separated. Deasy loped towards the market, looking about him, while Kelly went to Wilson's door. He knocked and called, 'All right!' Deasy, now moving down the street towards him, faltered. A tunic button glinted in a darkened recess. A peeler was standing in a doorway opposite Wilson's house. The door in front of Kelly opened and the two men slid in.

It was midnight before they re-emerged. They were halfway down the street before they noticed: the peeler was still there and stepped out of the shadows into a cone of light. A column of buttons glinted in the gaslight. Kelly drew Deasy to a halt at the corner of the street. There was no question of returning home. They'd be followed. Perhaps they could bluff their way out of it.

But before either could speak, the peeler lifted a steel

whistle to his lips. An urgent blast bounced down the streets. The clatter of heavy boots came from the Market.

'Is there a problem, officer?' Kelly's face was all bafflement.

'Stay there!' the advancing peeler ordered, pointing at their feet with an index finger.

The clattering boots slewed to a halt.

'These two are nicked, Sergeant Bears,' the peeler said to his panting colleague.

'Is this how the British government ...' Before Kelly could finish, Deasy hitched his coat and drew a revolver. The peelers lurched forward and, grunting and cursing, manhandled him to the ground.

In ten minutes the Fenian leaders were installed in the Albert Street police station cells, booked in as Mr Wright and Mr Williams, and charged with loitering.

***

Of all the disasters Kelly and Deasy had contemplated, this was the worst. The unifying and driving force of the Fenian movement was neutralised at a time when it was poised to enter a new and more dynamic phase of the campaign for national independence. The two most feared men in the British Empire had fallen into the hands of the authorities, apparently as a result of the suspicions of a single policeman acting entirely on his own initiative. But there was a chance that what the authorities had gained by good fortune they might now lose by incompetence.

During the first few days of their captivity there was nothing to suggest to the Fenian leaders that their captors realised who they were. There was no formal identification. The next day, Thursday 12 September, when the two appeared at Bridge Street magistrates' court, they were charged in their assumed names with loitering and remanded to the old city gaol, Belle Vue, in the township of Gorton on the city's periphery.

Within a few days, however, *The Manchester Guardian* informed its readers that the two men were in fact Kelly and Deasy. Detective McHale of G Division – counter-subversion – of the Dublin police arrived in Manchester to identify them and take them back to Dublin to stand trial for their role in the rising of March that year.

The loss of Kelly and Deasy was such a disastrous blow to the movement that those who now assumed leadership believed every possible means of rescuing them should be tried. Rescuing leading members from prison was already something of a Fenian speciality. Contrary to all expectations and to the enduring embarrassment of the authorities, the Fenians had extricated James Stephens from the recesses of Richmond Gaol. Apart from its practical benefits, a prison breakout had enormous psychological and symbolic importance. Nothing provided a greater boost to morale than defying the British government in the very seat and symbol of its power. Nothing so undermined its aura of invincibility.

So it was to be expected that the Fenians would try to rescue Kelly and Deasy. Yet this possibility does not seem to have occurred to the Manchester authorities until it happened. The British government liked to reassure the public that Fenian ineptitude rendered them incapable of posing a serious threat to the authority of the state. The Irish, they believed, lacked the discipline and orderliness of mind to enact their conspiracies with efficiency and rigour. The British, by contrast, had developed and mastered systems which were capable of achieving staggering results. How else was it possible, for instance, for a handful of civil servants and a few soldiers to rule a great subcontinent like India and its vast population? What chance did a bunch of 'low Irish' have of wresting the most wanted man in the Empire from the grasp of the authorities?

***

Condon sat in the Red Lion Inn across the road from the magistrates' court on Bridge Street and watched the routine of preparing remand prisoners for the journey to Belle Vue Prison. What he saw lifted his spirits. The police used a Black Maria – a secure police van with separate locked cubicles, pulled by dray horses – to transport prisoners. The policeman assigned to the court, Sergeant Charles Brett, placed the prisoners in the van, locked the door and then sat at the front with the driver. A third man, Constable Knox, a sixty-three-year-old ex-soldier, stood on the step at the back of the van. In all probability, Kelly and Deasy would be locked in one of the small cubicles, though not all prisoners were: when there were too many for each to

have a cell – as was frequently the case – they were packed
two to a cell and the remainder stood in the passageway.

September 1867 was not the first time Edward Condon had planned a rescue. After the abortive Canadian
venture of 1866, he had devised a plan to rescue one of
the captured Fenians, Michael Murphy. Murphy, however,
made the plan superfluous by effecting his own escape.
On that bright September day Condon walked the route
from Bridge Street Magistrates' Court – where Kelly and
Deasy were to appear on 18 September. As soon as he left
Ardwick Green by Hyde Road he saw a bridge which immediately struck him as the ideal spot for the rescue. Built
to carry the London and North Western Railway, its three
sturdy arches, one on each side for pedestrians and a large
one for vehicles, spanned Hyde Road. It was perfect. His
men would hide on the far side of the bridge and swoop
once the Black Maria emerged. They would grab Brett, get
the keys and subdue the driver and Knox. Condon would
then take Kelly and Deasy by cab to Ashton Road – which
ran parallel to Hyde Road and was less than a mile away
from the bridge – where another cab would be waiting to
take them to a safe house in Ashton-under-Lyne.

But before Condon got beyond the initial planning
stage there was a problem. The three Manchester centres,
Nolan, Neary and Lavery disagreed about who should take
part in the rescue. Nolan was adamant that it would be safer
to recruit men from outside the area as the Manchester
police could not readily identify them. Condon rejected

this. He had two reasons for insisting that Manchester men carry out the rescue, one practical and one to do with morale. First, he believed that after the rescue, as the men involved fled the scene, they would be at a serious disadvantage if they had no knowledge of the streets and ginnels that made parts of the city impenetrable warrens where the police dared not go. Second, choosing outsiders for the job would reflect badly on the Manchester men and damage their morale. Condon's opinion prevailed.

The next problem was weapons. When Condon asked the local men, they told him they had none and the sum total available to buy any was £1. He organised an emergency collection and sent Daniel Darragh to Birmingham to buy ten pistols.

The rescue was planned for Wednesday 18 September. That morning the men chosen to take part met for a final briefing in a house on Oldham Road. Many were pale and had clearly not slept. Though only about half were to receive weapons, each had a specific role to discharge and knew that the success of the plan and with it the entire future of the movement might depend on him.

Condon opened a Gladstone bag and scooped out a tangle of shirts and undergarments, scattering them across the table. One by one he drew out ten pistols and laid them out in a row. The smell of engine oil filled the room. He made two neat piles each of five cardboard boxes, the size of tobacco tins.

'Stay off the streets,' said Condon. Ten men took a gun.

One turned the weapon in his hands, inspecting it from all angles. Another rubbed the barrel in the palm of his hand. A third held it to his nostrils, inhaling the cold, harsh odour of the oil.

The men who stood around the table, on whom the fate of Fenianism depended, were a cross-section of the membership. Michael O'Brien, a thirty-year-old Irish-American veteran of the Civil War with the build of a middleweight, was relaxed. He had thick blonde hair and a good-natured smile that made the corners of his eyes crinkle. It was his default expression. Despite the tension in the room, his characteristic smile seldom left his face.

William Allen, only nineteen, couldn't stand still and rocked on the balls of his feet. His colour was high and there was something girlish about his smooth skin, high cheekbones and thick, black, curly hair. He was a man whose fine long fingers were as sensitive as his eyes. He balanced a gun in the flat of his hand, pondering its heft as he did that of the billiard cue he manipulated to such good effect in halls around the city. A joiner by trade, during the day his plane and chisel shaped timber.

Michael Larkin was a striking contrast to O'Brien. He looked much older than his thirty-two years and his pallor told of a man who was feeble with sickness. A wispy goatee heightened the puckish appearance of the little tailor, so stooped he looked even shorter than his five foot five inches. With Allen and O'Brien, he was charged with preventing anyone pursuing Kelly and Deasy.

The Manchester centres Lavery, Neary and Nolan were also there. John Neary was a long-term revolutionary. Like Stephens, he was a veteran of the 1848 rising, after which he escaped to Manchester where he established the St Patrick's Brotherhood. This organisation became a front for those attracted to revolutionary nationalism and played a key role in the development of Fenianism in the city. John Nolan was the head of the Ancient Order of Hibernians, another focus for nationalist sentiment.

Peter Ryan, another prominent Manchester Fenian present, was fanatical in his commitment to the movement. He volunteered to go to the magistrates' court and, should the opportunity arise, shoot the notorious spy Corydon.

Of the men there, Condon later identified one for special praise. Daniel Reddin of Dublin, was, according to Condon, one of the 'bravest and coolest men I ever met'. Not in receipt of Condon's commendation, however, was Thomas Bolger, whom Condon later blamed for everything that went wrong. His role was to wait in a cab near the magistrates' court until the Black Maria carrying Kelly and Deasy set off. He was then to drive ahead and warn the men at the bridge. Crucially, once there, he was to retain the cab near the bridge in order to take the Fenian leaders to Ashton Road. There they would rendezvous with John Brannon who was charged with the task of providing the cab to take Kelly and Deasy to Ashton. Bolger's failure to carry out his role was, according to Condon, the reason why so many Fenians were captured at the scene of the rescue.

Condon went through their roles one last time. Then Ricard O'Sullivan Burke spoke. 'Remember,' he said, 'don't shoot unless it's necessary.' The men concealed the guns in their clothes. 'But if you have to, don't hesitate.'

3

A DECLARATION OF WAR

A long wailing scream exploded in the cavern of the bridge. The men crouched against the abutment stiffened.

It came again, louder and nearer, bouncing out from the bridge over the path.

One of the men pulled his gun and stepped into the footpath. The screaming child, his mouth a perfect circle, slewed to a halt, his head a foot from the gun barrel. Wide eyes looked from the gun to the scar on the gunman's cheek and then back at the gun.

'Get outa here, ye wee scamp,' said the gunman.

'Yes, mister,' said the boy, twelve-year-old Walker, turning and sprinting back into the tunnel of the bridge, the way he'd come. The sound of his boots hissed around the vault of brickwork.

As the armed men on Hyde Road waited for the Black Maria their plan was already unravelling.

***

As the newspapers had anticipated, Inspector Williams of the Special Irish Branch – a counter-terrorism agency – appeared at the magistrates' court on 18 September and requested, on behalf of Scotland Yard, that the men who claimed to be Wright and Williams be further remanded because there was compelling evidence that they were in fact Kelly and Deasy, the Fenian leaders. The inspector had, he said, warrants for the two men relating to their involvement in the rising in Ireland that March.

Peter Ryan, looking down from the public gallery, where he stood pressed up against the others who had come to catch a glimpse of the infamous Fenians, had no occasion to draw his gun: Corydon did not appear. As Sergeant Charles Brett took the Fenians down to the holding cell, Ryan left to join the crowd waiting outside for a glimpse of the most dangerous criminals in the land.

***

It was five minutes past two and in the detective office in the town hall basement William Mellor was in a flap. The clerk had just received a telegram from Dublin addressed to Chief Detective Maybury. But Maybury was nowhere to be found. Having checked the office again and asked the other detectives if they'd seen him, Mellor became worried. Telegrams were important. And usually urgent. He decided to open it.

It was about the Fenian prisoners. Mellor walked back down the office to Inspector Garner's desk.

'It's about them Fenians,' Mellor said, passing the telegram over.

'OK,' said Garner. When the clerk turned and walked away, the detective dropped the telegram on his desk and returned to the form he was filling. After a few seconds he picked it up again and began to read it. Then, with his eyes still on it, he stood up and with his free hand lifted his jacket from the back of his chair.

***

As Condon waited at the bridge on Hyde Road, he choked back his rage. The rescue was turning into a burlesque.

The men had been sworn to secrecy but someone had talked. Some of those who had not been chosen to take part in the rescue, men on the periphery of the movement and even some bar-room patriots, had gathered at the bridge. From noon many had filled the bar of the Halfway House, a little beer house wedged under the bridge on the Belle Vue side. Drinking and playing cards they couldn't fail to attract attention. One of them, a dapper young man in a fashionable salt and pepper coat and chimney pot hat, had particularly caught the barmaid's eye as he stood looking out of the window, rising and falling on the balls of his feet.

They, and those who stood out on the footpath, had been noticed by some locals, curious to know what was going on. What's more, Condon was worried about two of the men. Neary had become ill as they awaited the Black Maria and Condon sent him away, telling him to give his gun to one of the others. But he was far more concerned about Larkin. The little tailor had only recently returned from Ireland, where he'd buried his father, and by the look of him he wouldn't be long after him. Sweat beaded on his waxy forehead and his skin had taken on a sepulchral hue. Condon wanted him to go home but he would have none of it: he would do his duty, whatever the cost.

***

By 2.15 p.m. Inspector Garner had given up hope of finding Maybury in the crowd outside the magistrates' court. Then he spotted Superintendent Gee's brown Derby, half a head above the spectators, and elbowed a path to him.

As Gee peered at the telegram, a cry went up and shouts of 'Stand back!' and 'He's got a knife!' In the centre of a circle of spectators a constable and a civilian, locked at the wrists and bent double, wrestled. Garner shouldered his way through the crowd and kicked the civilian's legs from under him, causing him to fall on his stomach. He stamped his boot on the hand with the knife, pinning it to the cobbles.

Thus disabled was Francis McAuliffe, a Walter Mitty character with a genius for self-publicity. Tall, athletic and imposing, he frequently dressed as a priest and claimed various prestigious titles. Among other things, he maintained that while fighting for the pope, Garibaldi's troops had captured and imprisoned him for several months. Previously charged with Fenianism, the only evidence against him were the words of his public lectures and consequently the court discharged him. Subsequently he complained bitterly to the newspapers of his treatment and, much given to litigation, announced his intention to pursue his grievances through the courts until he was awarded considerable damages.

Entirely on his own initiative, McAuliffe had decided that single-handedly and armed with only a knife he would rescue the Fenian leaders. What he achieved was to convince the Manchester police that they should implement additional security measures.

***

In all the years he'd been doing the job this was the first time Sergeant Brett had travelled inside the Black Maria. Thousands of times he had ferried from the magistrates' court to Belle Vue Prison the pickpockets, prostitutes and drunks who passed through the system every day. Most he knew by name, and they called him 'Charlie'. Whether they were professional criminals – his 'regulars' – or simply unfortunates, he treated them all with the same courtesy. Always humane and decent, he was no soft touch, as one street ragamuffin discovered when he shouted abuse at Brett as he rode through the city on the Black Maria. Presumably confident that the sergeant would not abandon his post, the urchin called insults and taunts at the policeman. Brett at first seemed oblivious to the harangue until the Black Maria slowed to take a corner. Brett leaped to the pavement to a cacophony of whistles and cheers and sped after the boy, who with flailing arms and legs sought to outrun the greying peeler. On and on the boy ran, along Deansgate, in and out of ginnels and courts, the sound of the sergeant's boots getting steadily nearer until Brett grasped his collar in his fist.

The sergeant didn't haul the boy before a court. Nor did he cuff him or drive his substantial boot into his buttocks. There was no need: the boy's abject, cowering pleas, his frantic tears and sobs of entreaty had robbed him of all credibility. Brett was not a man for driving people so far down that they had no way back.

The sergeant was one of those rare people who enjoy the good opinion of everyone they encounter. His superiors regarded him as efficient and conscientious and within a criminal justice system that was often harsh, he was always the face of humanity.

Now Superintendent Gee told him that he was to lock himself inside the Maria. Whether it was the telegram warning of a possible Fenian rescue or McAuliffe's inept rescue bid that had alarmed Gee is unclear. Whatever the reason, he decided that the sooner the Manchester police deposited the Fenians in Belle Vue Prison the better.

In addition to Kelly and Deasy, each locked in a separate cell and handcuffed, the van contained other prisoners: a twelve-year-old boy, Joseph Partington, sentenced to a period in an industrial school, and three female prisoners, all petty criminals – Emma Halliday, Ellen Cooper and

Frances Armstrong – who stood in the narrow corridor with Sergeant Brett. The three women were known to Brett, some of his 'regulars'. Six policemen including Constables George Shaw, Seth Bromley, John Taylor and William Yarwood took their positions on top of the van with sixty-three-year-old Constable Matthew Knox and Constable Connell both standing on the step. Charles Pollitt drove. Another four constables followed behind in a cab driven by James Worthington.

The Black Maria and the cab clattered out of the yard and onto the cobbles of Bridge Street. The crowd immediately began to disperse.

Fifty yards away Bolger's cab pulled out of a side street into the snaking traffic. It was exactly 3.30 in the afternoon.

***

At the bridge on Hyde Road Condon shook his head. As he looked towards Belle Vue Prison, he could see the retreating backs of Michael O'Brien and three women. As if taking their Sunday afternoon constitutional, the ladies had chanced along and spotting O'Brien fell into giggling and chattering with him. The van was due any second and to get the women out of the way Condon had told O'Brien to take them to the Justice Birch, a pub directly opposite the gates of the gaol.

While Condon was still watching the four figures moving towards the pub, he heard the grind of steel rims on cobbles. He looked round the abutment and saw Bolger leaning out of the hansom cab. The Black Maria was fifty yards behind him. The men braced themselves. Many pressed their backs up against the bridge. Others stood, frozen, their arms cocked with stones in their hands. Some drew weapons from coats and waistbands and held them pointed at the maw of the bridge. The clacking of hooves on stone grew louder and then echoed in the tunnel of the bridge.

The Illustrated London News *depiction of the rescue*
Courtesy of Mercier Archives

As the horses emerged at the other side a great roar went up, tangled with screams and the thud of stones against the hollow Black Maria. The peelers cowered, their arms protecting their heads. One had his hat shot away at the same instant as a stone hit him on the shoulder, throwing him back where he momentarily teetered, then fell to the cobbles on his head.

A man with a gun stood, knees bent, in the middle of the road. The horses baulked under the bombardment of stones and as the near-side animal reared, baring its teeth, the gunman straightened his arm and shot it in the neck. The horse bucked, its eyes wild, a rich stain glistening on its dun coat. It hit the cobbles, legs splayed, the hole in its neck bubbling blood. Its partner bucked in terror, its neck arched back, bending the shaft, popping one of the traces and spattering the chain links over the road. Before the second horse's feet hit the ground, the gunman shot the animal twice between the forequarters, sending it sprawling in a belly flop, eyes wild in terror and incomprehension.

Pockets of fighting flared under and all around the bridge. Men fought and threatened, brandished weapons, advanced and retreated in five or six simultaneous battles, each oblivious to the others. The air was thick with stones and jagged bricks, gunpowder and animal blood. As in a medieval battle, men wielded brutal weapons and hacked at each other with boots and fists. Each man identified his foe and tackled him, seeing nothing else.

Constable Yarwood, defying the bricks that exploded at

his feet and weaving like a flyweight, ran towards the gunman and launched a stone which snapped his head back and split the flesh on the point of his chin. In one unbroken movement the peeler knocked the gunman's hand up with his forearm and dashing towards the toll bar on the far side of the bridge vaulted it like a champion hurdler, leaped into the cab which Bolger, contrary to instructions, had abandoned, and raced towards Belle Vue Prison. The gunman, wiping the blood from his chin with the back of one hand and trying to control the shake in the other, fired after him.

Condon ran to the back of the Black Maria. The peelers in the cab leaped down, their boots ringing on the cobbles, and also moved, tentatively, towards the van. Two gunmen confronted them in the middle of the road.

'Get back or I'll stretch yous all. Get back, damn ye,' roared one of the gunmen. He lifted his hand and fired two shots into the top of the bridge. The noise bounced around the chamber of the bridge and a puff of brick dust danced in the November sunlight. The peelers flinched, but held their ground.

Again he levelled the gun. He squinted down the length of the barrel, lining it up with a peeler's shoulder.

'Get back, I tell you.' His voice was calm and low. Two constables fixed him in their stare. Their glare said, 'You'd better kill us because we won't forget you.' He squeezed the trigger. One peeler shuddered, but did not call out. No one moved. He trained the gun on the other constable. He fired. The man howled and clutched his groin. At this point the two peelers bolted, the first clutching his shoulder, blood staining the gap between his fingers, the second hopping in his wake.

The policemen atop the Black Maria tried to kick away the men who were scrambling up. Straining backwards, their hands flat by their buttocks, they gripped the top of the van, their feet flailing. Under another deluge the peelers cowered against the thump of stone and brick on flesh and skull. There was a roar and a charge. Two pairs of arms wrestled a pair of legs to inertia and then yanked on them. The peeler catapulted forward, his arms crumpling under him as they broke his fall.

A third cascade of stones finally routed the peelers from the Black Maria. They fled through the arch of the bridge as shots boomed over their heads. At the side of the van, grey-haired Constable Knox lay pinned to the cobbles.

'Where are the keys?' a man with a ribboned hat roared, his knee on the peeler's breastbone, his hands choking the blood from his throat up into his bursting face. Knox's coat was pulled up under his armpits, exposing a flash of white shirt against the dark uniform. Groaning like a wounded ox, his body rocking from side to side, the peeler wrestled with the wrists pressed up under his chin.

'The keys, or I'll tear the head offa ye.'

'In the van,' Knox panted, 'with Brett … in the van.'

Inside the Black Maria the women were howling, their hands scraping their hair back from their faces. The skin of the van acted like a drum. Tossed from side to side they pressed their backs to the narrow passage and wedged their feet against the wall opposite. Sergeant Charles Brett bent to look through the ventilator which was a quarter of the way down the door. 'It's them Fenians!' he gasped.

'Jesus Christ, Charlie, they'll slaughter us all,' shrieked one of the women.

'Ladies, ladies, keep still,' said Brett, his face ashen over his luxuriant beard. The whimpering abated. 'They can't get in,' he said, rattling the keys at his hip.

Brett hunkered down, placed the heels of his hands on the bottom corners of the latticed vent, and with his elbows locked, pushed the weight of his body against his rigid arms.

The chuck, chuck, chuck of an axe rattled the door.

'Leave that,' said a voice on the other side of the door, as clear as if he was in the van. 'Open this thing.' There was a resounding thud and Brett's body shuddered as he pushed down on his extended arms. He groaned and bent his head to his arms as he pressed down on the vent. Another thud, the vent shot up and Brett's elbows bent as a stone rammed between the slats of the vent and wedged it open. A gun barrel poked through.

On the road outside the crowd was growing. Drinkers from the nearby pubs spilled onto the paths. A big man named Sprosson at the front of the crowd turned to those behind him. He spoke in a forced voice. 'They won't shoot,' Sprosson said as he stepped forward, 'they haven't got the gumption.'

There was a rumble of approval from the crowd as they inched through the arch towards the van. Two gunmen stood full square to them in the middle of the road, legs wide apart, right arms crooked with the guns pointing to the grey sky. 'Keep back,' said the smaller of the two, levelling his gun.

The crowd stopped. Sprosson turned his head ninety degrees, looked to the front and then took a step forward. He was no more than four yards from the gun now pointing straight at his head. 'Not another inch.' Though the voice was barely above a whisper, they all heard it. No one moved. Sprosson could feel the eyes of the crowd boring into his back.

'Get back,' said one of the gunmen. His hand was steady. The other was wincing with the effort of keeping the gun still at the end of his quivering arm.

'Or else?' The big man turned round to display his sneer to those behind.

Boom. The shot exploded. Sprosson shrieked. The crowd turned and fled.

'Cowardly bastards,' wailed Sprosson, lying on the ground, clutching his ankle in both his hands. 'Come back you cowardly bastards,' he shrieked.

The women in the van were now silent, the only sound was their laboured breathing.

'Hand out those keys!' called an invisible voice behind the gun at the slatted grill.

'No, I'll do my duty to the last,' declared Brett.

'Give me out those keys!' repeated the voice.

'Come away, Charlie,' shrieked one of the women, Ellen Cooper, pulling at Brett's arm. The sergeant tried to shrug her off then lurched back towards the grill. A shot exploded. Their ears rang and the van filled with screams and the stench of burning chemicals.

'He's killed!' shrieked Cooper. Brett lay sprawled against the door, his face a veil of gore.

'Hand out the keys!' The voice was now shrill.

'I will, I will.' Cooper unhooked the hoop from Brett's belt and passed it through the grill. The door opened and Brett tumbled out backwards.

'Out! Out!' A man with high cheekbones gestured towards the open door. They cowered under the weapon and leaped from the top of the steps out into the cool air.

'Where's the colonel?' demanded the man. A volley of stones hit the Black Maria. He turned back to the door. The mob had advanced to the mouth of the bridge and was stoning those around the van. Two shots rang out under the bridge. The crowd faltered but were soon edging forward again.

'Peelers from the prison!' The cry went up all around the van, 'Peelers from the prison.'

The man in the doorway of the Black Maria scrutinised the thick bunch of keys in his hand.

Ten yards away some warders – turnkeys from Belle Vue – leaped down from the moving cab. They shouldered their way to the front of the crowd until they faced the

Sergeant Charles Brett
Courtesy of Mercier
Archives

gunmen across a gap no wider than a weaving shed and littered with stones.

'Get back,' said one of the gunmen. 'Get back, I say.' He stepped back as he spoke, levelled the gun and then fired two shots above their heads. Though the turnkeys bobbed, their arms above their heads, they continued to edge forward, with the crowd close behind them.

In the doorway of the Black Maria, Allen clasped Kelly round the shoulders. 'Kelly, I'll die for you before I'll give you up.'

'Get these off,' said Kelly, raising his cuffed hands. He and Deasy blinked like miners after a shift.

Kelly stretched the chain across the top of the van step

and one of the Fenians strained and grunted, trying to prize apart the links with a cleaver. A cheer from the mob under the bridge made them turn round. Peelers brandishing sabres were jumping down from a horse-bus.

'Get over the wall,' said Condon, pointing to a where a six-foot brick wall, running from the mouth of the bridge, separated the footpath from a railway goods yard.

A roar went up like a crowd greeting the off at a race meeting. The mob surged forward, flooding out from under the bridge, swamping the Fenians around the van. The thud of boot on ribs, the plock of truncheon on skull, the crack of nose gristle crushed by a blow, filled the air.

Kelly and Deasy levered their bodies up onto the wall and dropped down into the yard. They scrambled across the railway tracks just before a long goods train snaked by, preventing pursuit. Allen, Larkin, O'Brien and Condon scaled the wall behind their leaders. They grappled their comrades onto the edging stones and pushed them over. Then they kicked out and used the guns as clubs to keep the mob at bay. The last wagon of the train passed as they jumped from the wall and ran across the yard.

The throng was behind them. Allen loped away into the distance, his effortless stride soon carrying him across the yard to a wall on the far side.

Larkin could barely raise his legs. His coughed as he stumbled along.

'Come on, for Christ's sake, Mikey,' called O'Brien, pulling him by the arm.

The mob's pent-up anger, heartened by the turnkeys and the peelers, swept all before it. As one Fenian was isolated and encircled, they beat and kicked him from all sides until he dropped, coiled into the foetal position and stiffened himself against each blow.

The rest fled, terror pumping their legs. The threat of being kicked to death routed all plans. But the mob was spreading out in all directions. O'Brien yanked Larkin from his knees and turned to face the warders. 'Get back or I'll stretch you.' He fired a shot into the ground in front of them, yet the crowd moved on relentlessly. They knew if he was going to shoot them he'd have done it by now.

He stumbled away, firing the gun over his head until it gave a hollow cough. Tottering to his knees, he tossed the pistol from him and lifted his arms. In one flowing movement, the warders pushed him face down, wedged their boots in his neck and pinioned his hands.

As Allen leaped from the wall into a street at the far side of the yard his feet shot from under him as they hit the cobbles, pitching him onto the broad of his back, legs skyward. The narrow street echoed to the ring of his boots and his gasp.

He lay motionless. A shawled woman, the toes of her clogs sniffing the air, stared down at him. He straightened his back. As if seeing it for the first time, he stared at the gun. Slowly, he opened his hand and let it roll onto the cobbles. She squeezed a fistful of shawl under her chin.

Allen was winded and steadied himself against the wall.

Taking several shuddering draughts of air he straightened his back just as someone dropped on him from the top of the wall, crumpling him to the cobbles. His assailant smashed him on the back of the skull with the butt of the discarded gun, pummelling him frenziedly.

The woman's screams brought people rushing into the road. They dragged Allen from under his assailant just as the peelers appeared at the top of the wall.

***

An hour later, Condon was in the centre of Manchester. He and Miles Brennan had escaped to a nearby safe house where Condon had shaved off his moustache and changed his clothes. He had no idea if Kelly and Deasy had made it to the safe house prepared as their first hiding place. So he and John Nugent went to a nearby livery stable to hire a horse and carriage so they could check whether the Fenian leaders were safe.

They were met with hostility and suspicion: the story of the rescue had spread round the city. They left on foot for the city centre, hoping to get a tram to Ashton. By the time they reached Oldham Road, every corner seemed to have its own peeler. Some stood on their toes, scanning the passers-by. When the crowds started to thin out Condon realised they were being followed.

'Cross over,' said Condon and stepped into the road. They dodged between two oncoming cabs and turned down a side street. Before they were twenty yards from the main road they heard steps behind them. They carried on walking at the same pace, reached a street that ran parallel to Oldham Road and walked back towards the city centre.

The steps were still there, quickening.

'You keep walking,' said Condon. He stopped and turned.

'What do you want?' Condon demanded. The two men had the athletic look of military men. They were soldiers – or detectives.

'Stop there,' said the one with the tweed jacket and Derby. Pedestrians on the far side of the road gawked at them.

'That man is a Fenian,' said the detective, drawing a cosh from inside his jacket and pointing it at Condon. 'Stop him.'

Condon turned and ran. Ten strides on he entered a side street, the sound of boots clattering behind him, before he realised it was a blind alley.

He sprinted for the wall at the end. With a fear-fuelled leap his hands might reach the top. People were in the street, between him and the wall. He evaded outstretched arms, skipping past like a rugby fullback. But just as he thought he'd evaded the last man, a boot caught him on the shin, slewing him across the cobbles into the foot of the wall. Two fat women moved from a doorway towards him. He tried to rise but they fell on him, pinning him to the ground, burying him in a reek of sweat and stale beer.

Of Nugent, however, there was no sign. Like Kelly and Deasy, he had disappeared.

4

MANHUNT

Every policeman in the country was after them. It was the most extensive manhunt ever launched in Britain. And if the efforts of the constabularies weren't enough to find Thomas Kelly and Timothy Deasy, the reward money ensured that every member of the public was the eyes and ears of the government.

The police notice offering a reward of £300 for information leading to the arrest of Kelly or Deasy made it unlikely that any outside Fenian circles would help the fugitives. At a time when even the most frugal working people lived a precarious existence from one meagre wage to the next, capturing either of the Fenian leaders guaranteed financial security. To put this in context, at that time a Manchester labourer fortunate enough to find employment for most of the year would earn about £50. In other words, a reward of £300 was equal to about six years' earnings. There was also a reward of £200 for information leading to the arrest of anyone who attacked the van.

The Times smugly predicted that the Fenian leaders

would soon be back in custody. The newspaper had ample reason for confidence. Leaving aside the reward money, Kelly and Deasy were the most detested men in the country. What's more, they were highly conspicuous. Anyone who caught a glimpse of Kelly's ready smile would identify what the wanted poster described as 'one tooth missing from the right side of his upper jaw'. Deasy also had a distinguishing, though less conspicuous, feature: a scar just under his ear on his right cheek.

Even if no member of the public spotted them, the authorities boasted that the Fenian movement was riddled with spies and informers. The fugitives could trust no one. A lethal cocktail of English nationalism and greed made every stranger a threat to them and convinced the authorities that they wouldn't be free for long.

But the Fenian leaders were no ordinary criminal fugitives. Their background gave them the determination and guile which were to prove their greatest assets.

The English newspapers delighted in describing Fenian prisoners as 'low Irish', shorthand for everything English racial and class prejudice detested. For the benefit of those not able to interpret the code, they explained that those accused of Fenian activity were 'of no education' or of 'imperfect education'. This fitted in with the most popular explanation of support for Fenianism, according to which the Irish were a simple-minded, largely illiterate people, given to unreasonable resentment of their English benefactors and prey to the machinations of scheming troublemakers. The reality, however, didn't square with this fantasy.

Kelly and Deasy, articulate, intelligent men of action, bore no relation to the caricature Fenian. Kelly was a man shaped by the privation of his early life, his experience as a journalist and newspaper proprietor in the rough and tumble of nineteenth-century American politics and the abrasive culture of trade union conflict in the burgeoning cities of the northern states. He'd commanded men with distinction in a brutal mechanised war that pushed those caught up in it to the limits of physical and psychological endurance. Underpinning and giving meaning to all these experiences were a profound religious faith and an incandescent passion for his country. He and Deasy were clever, tough and resourceful men of the world. But in the eyes of the British public they were the embodiment of evil and a threat to security, order and sound government.

It was during the American Civil War that the Fenian spectre first came to haunt the British public and soon any mention of them in the press was sufficient to create a shudder of fear and revulsion. It began with the *New York Mercury*'s sensational exposé of the Fenian Brotherhood in 1863, which was then taken up by the papers on the other side of the Atlantic.

After the Chester Castle raid and the rising in Ireland in March 1867, the British public was acutely aware of the threat the Fenians posed. Prompted by daily press reports, the public was in a state of high anxiety and ever vigilant for Fenians in their midst. Additionally, the fugitives had one great handicap which was enough to outweigh all their advantages of experience and temperament. It was their Irish-American accents. In our day of American films and easy inter-continental travel, American slang and even an American twang are commonplace. In the Manchester of the 1860s, a three-piece suit emblazoned with the stars and stripes would have been no more conspicuous. The local people spoke a variety of the distinctive Lancashire dialect almost incomprehensible to outsiders. As soon as they opened their mouths Kelly and Deasy would betray themselves.

What's more, the full resources of the government were directed against them as the authorities tried to retrieve some credibility from what was a grossly embarrassing fiasco. At all levels, from the Home Office down, the government and the police were mortified by their escape. With the sole exception of Sergeant Charles Brett, no one charged with responsibility for the two most dangerous men in the Empire came out of the affair in a good light. It is impossible to exaggerate the government's discomfort and its critics were soon demanding answers. How was it possible that such a rescue could take place in broad daylight in the centre of an English city? Why had the Manchester police ignored the warning from Ireland that a rescue was about to take place? Why were the prisoners not properly guarded by sufficient armed officers to deter a rescue bid or at least to repel it? Why had the government not taken steps to ensure that the prisoners were safe by sending specialist detectives from London to organise their transfer to Ireland? After all, it was not as if the government had not already suffered the indignity of losing a Fenian leader. It was not long since James Stephens had apparently evaporated from Richmond Gaol, which the authorities had boasted was impregnable. To lose one Fenian leader was perhaps unfortunate, but to lose two more looked very much like incompetence.

Certainly, Lord Mayo – chief secretary for Ireland and in effect the British government in the province – was apoplectic with rage. He had warned the Manchester police that a rescue was afoot. The failure of the authorities in England to take adequate precautions merely confirmed Mayo's low opinion of those responsible for countering subversion in Britain.

The home secretary, Gathorne Gathorne-Hardy, was no less incensed. His diary entry for 18 September makes it clear that he too was scandalised by the audacity of the rescue and appalled by the incompetence of the Manchester police. No doubt his anger was in part fuelled by the knowledge that there were both allies and opponents who would blame his government, claiming that it was their failure to deal firmly with the Fenians involved in the rising of March 1867 that was the root cause of the latest outrage. Surely, his opponents argued, executions in March would have shown the rebels that they could not with impunity oppose the legitimate authority of the state.

The only way the government might retrieve any credibility was by quickly recapturing Kelly and Deasy.

Their most likely escape route was through the port of Liverpool on one of the ocean-going vessels which carried emigrants from every country in Europe to America. All routes between Manchester and Liverpool were under surveillance. Every passenger boarding ship in the port did so under the suspicious eye of the police.

Nor was there any lack of information from the public. It was clear that the British masses were vigilant. Perhaps too vigilant. Soon after the escape it was reported that the fugitives were in Bradford and that Deasy was still wearing the handcuffs in which he had escaped. Apparently, Kelly had gone into the house of one Daniel Rider and, seeking not to raise suspicion, made no reference to the handcuffs but instead asked for the loan of a tool to remove nails from his boots. Rider raised the alarm but both men escaped. Later, however, in speaking to the gentlemen of the press, Rider made no mention of how Kelly was shod. Popular mythology had it that all Americans wore square-toed boots, which were then fashionable on the far side of the Atlantic. It was said that Dublin Castle spies were able to identify American Fenians by the style of their footwear. According to a tale popular at the time, an Irish mother, hoping to avoid attracting the attention of the authorities, wrote to her son in America: 'For God's sake, son, don't be wearing any of them square toe boots when you come home to visit.'

In the frenzy of anti-Fenian fever that swept the country sightings were reported every day. The day after the rescue, neighbours reported their suspicions when gunfire was heard from a house in Manchester. Armed police stormed the building only to find that a drunk had inadvertently discharged a shotgun. He explained that he'd bought the gun to protect himself 'against those damn Fenians', but hadn't yet mastered it.

Three days after the rescue, the Manchester police were convinced they had trapped their quarry. The residents of Every Street in Hulme were alerted to the Fenians in their midst by suspicious nocturnal comings and goings. Armed police and soldiers surrounded the suspect house. When voices from behind the barricaded doors refused them entry, they screwed up their courage and broke in, watched by a large crowd hoping to catch a glimpse of the fearful Fenians.

They emerged with what the press described as 'a puny man and two women' found cowering in a room. The house had no furniture but contained 'a mass of correspondence', which, it was implied, would lay bare the inner workings of the Fenian conspiracy. Upon investigation, however, it became clear that most of this correspondence related to the occupants' rent arrears. The 'puny man' had barricaded the house against forcible eviction. The police found nothing more incriminating and released him.

If all the reports are to be believed, Kelly and Deasy were certainly getting around. On 24 September they called into a barber's in Halifax, presumably trying to alter their distinctive appearance. In the police descriptions, Kelly had a moustache and a squared-off beard of the type fashionable among fighting men during the American Civil War. The same day Kelly was reported in Nottingham, heading in the direction of Narrow Marsh, the town's Irish quarter. On the same day *The Irish Times* reported the escape of another Fenian, a prisoner from Clonmel prison. It seems the authorities were having difficulty keeping the Fenians they had, let alone capturing those they'd misplaced.

The next day it was reported that Kelly was in Dover, organising an attack on the castle. The mayor was so alarmed he purchased a supply of arms for the police who searched the town and every steamer leaving for the continent. Undaunted, the indefatigable Kelly kept moving.

The *Glasgow Herald* of 26 September reported that the fugitives had been traced to the Sussex Hotel, London Bridge, where they had slept on the night of their escape. It was said they had travelled to Dover by train and escaped to France. If so, they managed to evade the French authorities as there was no sign of them on the other side of the Channel.

At last the Manchester police believed their luck had changed. They received information from Hull that two men, who gave their names as Kelly and Deasy, were on board *The Panther*. Detectives rushed across the country, arriving just as the steamer was about to leave port. However, the startled captives were able to assure the police that they were bona fide businessmen who had nothing to do with the Fenians and were in fact 'two gentlemen, both loyal to the backbone'.

On the same day the authorities received a tip-off that Kelly was aboard a Waterford-bound steamer. For several weeks every ship in and out of the port of Liverpool was searched but no sign of the Fenians was found. The Waterford-bound vessel proved no different.

On 7 October an unfortunate Scotsman had his holiday in Shrewsbury rudely interrupted when he was arrested and subjected to several hours' interrogation. Eventually he convinced police that though he fitted the description of Kelly, his Scots accent was not a cunning ruse to hide a Yankee drawl.

'Kelly captured in Cheadle', a headline of 11 October trumpeted. A few days later the police had to admit that the poor unfortunate they had arrested had nothing to do with the Fenians.

The lack of police progress is amazing and it appears the only people troubled by police activity were holidaymakers. An American artist, Mr De Poix Tyrel of Wolverhampton, was seized in Neath because of his accent, and another man, visiting relations in Salford, was taken into custody because he resembled the police description of Deasy.

Then, on 27 October, five weeks after the Manchester rescue, the *City of Paris*, out of Liverpool via Cobh, arrived in New York. Among its passengers was Timothy Deasy. A few days later his supporters held an extravagant reception banquet in his honour. The news from America, however, made no mention of Kelly and it was assumed that he was still in England. The story of Deasy's escape was reported in the British press and enraged the authorities.

According to Deasy's account, Kelly and he had fled from the prison van to the nearby home of an old Irish woman. Having changed their clothes and returned to the streets to mingle with the curious crowds, they slipped into Manchester and then to Liverpool from where he'd taken ship to America. But before that, they had had a number of audacious escapes.

According to Deasy, shortly after the rescue, Kelly had boarded a Manchester tram and took his seat only to discover that six policemen were upstairs arresting two suspected Fenians. On another occasion Kelly ran into a group of policemen and asked what all the excitement was about. They obligingly told him all about the dangerous Fenians who'd escaped. But, according to Deasy, Kelly saved his most audacious antics for the police monitoring Liverpool docks.

As the fugitives approached the steamer, the *City of Paris*, they saw a line of detectives scrutinising the passengers as they went up the gangplank. Kelly was posing as a porter, carrying the bags of the disguised Deasy. The detectives allowed them to pass. But this, according to Deasy, was not good enough for Kelly, who wanted to inject a little excitement into the situation.

Kelly, so the story went, started a row with Deasy,

pretending to take offence at the meagre tip he'd been given and demanding the other porters support him in his complaint. The exchange became so heated that the detectives threatened to arrest Kelly unless he went on his way. The surly porter slouched down the gangway and returned to Liverpool, where he had unfinished business.

Deasy's account is the stuff of a mischievous mind, so good that it deserves to be true. Most of it is fantasy, devised to taunt the English. But the authorities were convinced that one part of it *was* true and that Kelly was still in England. Letters from someone purporting to be Kelly began to turn up in the Irish press. And at the beginning of December the authorities received information that convinced them that the Fenian leader was still within their grasp.

Police spies told them that the Shamrock beer house, near the centre of Manchester, was the focus of suspicious activity. The pub was as a consequence kept under observation for a number of weeks. Then an army of police, under the command of top-ranking officers, gathered for the kill. By the time they were ready to act a large and hostile crowd of locals had assembled. But the police were not to be deterred. They burst in and seized everyone in the place. Among them were Fenian sympathisers previously arrested and released. But there was no sign of Kelly or Deasy.

The police were running out of ideas. Some were even beginning to believe a story circulating since the day of the escape – that the cunning Fenians had masqueraded as a wedding party. On his escape from the van Kelly had taken the role of the groom. The bride was said to be Mary Ann Hickey's sister. Mary Ann was the sweetheart of William Allen, one of the men who faced a capital charge because of his role in the rescue. According to this story, the happy couple left Manchester by train and boarded a ship for America that very day.

Then the authorities' worst fears were confirmed. News reached England that Kelly had indeed arrived in America. And the truth of his escape was almost as sensational as the story Deasy had concocted to bate the British government.

Kelly had hidden in Manchester for several months, moving from one safe house to another. He spent many days in the home of an eminent dentist, his namesake, Dr Kelly, who occupied a splendid house on Oxford Road, one of the main roads leading out to the south of the city. The police were suspicious of Dr Kelly and raided the house. As they ransacked the building, the Fenian leader hid in a water cistern on the roof. He knew they would be back and so he moved to another safe house in Cheetham Hill, to the north of the city centre. Soon after arriving, he heard that the police were on to him and were in the process of sealing off the area.

Only his courage and the help of a sympathetic priest saved him. He swapped clothes with Fr Tracy and strode out into the street, warmly greeting the police as they closed in. He then made his way to the home of a Fenian who worked for a wine merchant. Kelly remained there for a number of days until his host smuggled him out of the city. Hidden between casks of wine destined for Liverpool docks he managed to avoid detection by police who were watching all traffic into the city. But the docks were also under close scrutiny.

Fortunately, the Liverpool Fenians included Egan, a ship's joiner. He was employed to fit out berths in the numerous emigrant ships leaving Albert Dock every week. He managed to smuggle Kelly onto a ship, disguised as a carpenter's mate, and then sealed him up inside a hollow bulkhead. Undetected and fed by a Fenian member of the crew, he reached Queenstown (Cobh), the last port of call before New York. Once at sea the sailor released him from his temporary prison and he reached America after an uneventful voyage.

In truth, it is impossible to be sure exactly how Kelly and Deasy managed to avoid capture and eventually escape. The waters have been muddied, sometimes deliberately. Deasy's account, given on arrival in New York, was clearly designed to mislead the British authorities: to tell the truth about their escape would have endangered the organisation and those who had helped them.

As the years passed the story of the escape became a part of Fenian lore. It's hard to imagine that those recounting such an adventure were always able to resist the temptation to embellish such a good story. At the very least they may have omitted the less exciting phases of the escapade.

Many years later a newspaper correspondent, John Smethurst, claimed knowledge of Kelly and Deasy's whereabouts during the period when they were most vulnerable, immediately after their escape. An acquaintance of Smethurst's, a Mr Aldred, had discovered his father's diaries for the years 1835 to 1910. They tell of Kelly and Deasy hiding in the crypt of All Saints church, Barton, a dozen miles from Manchester. Young Aldred took them food until it was safe to smuggle them away in a canal boat to Runcorn. There is nothing improbable about this story, but neither is there anything to corroborate it.

However they did it, Kelly and Deasy escaped and at no time did the authorities have any idea of their whereabouts. This is one of the most remarkable aspects of the whole story. Yet it's an aspect never adequately explained. If the British authorities are to be believed, their disappearance is inexplicable. One reason *The Times* was so confident of their speedy recapture was the common belief that the whole Fenian movement was riddled with informers. After all, Dublin Castle managed to plant their man, Pierce Nagle, in the offices of the *Irish People*, the hub of the movement. His information had enabled the authorities to largely nullify the rising of March 1867. Everyone who was well informed on the Fenian threat knew that spies such as John Joseph Corydon had played a major role in weakening the movement. They were valuable not least because of their ability to identify suspects not known to the local police and proved extremely useful in the wake of the Fenian rescue. When the authorities discovered that there was a plan afoot to murder them they whisked them away to a secure location. Yet, while Corydon was undeniably valuable to the police, the authorities' claims that they were party to all the inner workings of the Fenian movement are far from the truth.

What's more, there was a major difference between the organisation in Ireland and in Britain. The ideals of Fenianism were particularly attractive to emigrants. The prevailing attitude among them is neatly summed up in their describing themselves as exiles. They tended to regard leaving Ireland not as an opportunity to improve themselves economically and socially, but as a curse, inflicted on them by British misrule and repression. Once they arrived in the great industrial cities they became far more radical than their counterparts back home, far more committed to a cause which held out the prospect of a fairer, more just Ireland, in which they and all the other dispossessed would be restored to their rightful place on the land.

When the organisation was smashed in Ireland, it remained intact in Britain. This is shown by the secret convention held in Manchester in July 1867, at which both Kelly's and Deasy's leadership was affirmed, and their subsequent rescue from police custody. The Fenians in exile reaffirmed their radicalism by appointing Kelly, by excluding the squabbling Americans and by their decision to make Manchester the movement's headquarters. Their radicalism also cut them off from respectable society –

the Fenians were almost entirely working men forming a tightly knit group, as Lord Mayo frequently pointed out to the government in London.

What is clear, however, is that the news that Kelly was safely in New York and being fêted by Irish-America was a further blow to Home Secretary Gathorne-Hardy, Lord Mayo and Manchester's Chief Constable, William Palin. Now that the Fenian leaders were out of the reach of the British authorities the focus of their efforts shifted.

Palin knew there was only one way in which he might salvage his reputation. He was determined to bring to trial all those involved in the rescue. He had been on leave the day of the rescue but he realised that this did not reduce his accountability for what had happened. Nor did he seek to put the blame on others. Instead, from his base in Stanley Street police station, he took personal responsibility for the round-up of suspects. The Fenian leaders had escaped but those who had rescued them would not. It was to these men that the police now turned their attention.

5

'WILD PANIC'

The soft, yellow light from the Harp and Shamrock splashed an oily stain on the uneven footpath of Rochdale Road. The alehouse doors were thrown open and shouts from the bar filled the night air. The drinkers spilled out from the area around the bar, across the benches and stools, standing in tight clusters along the walls.

'A drink for all these on me, landlord,' cried a fat man, his billycock hat pushed back from his damp brow.

'Fair play to the man who shares his good fortune,' cried another, pummelling him on the back. A cheer went up and a dozen hands thrust their empty glasses towards the bar.

All the talk at the bar had been of the Manchester races until they'd heard of events on Hyde Road that afternoon. News of the rescue had run as fast as any of that day's winners. Great shifting crowds had gathered in the city centre, a gabbling mass of humanity swarming from the Town Hall on Cross Street the 300 yards to Market Street and back again, growing and changing as it moved along, sending out to every corner of the city the news that Kelly and Deasy were free.

There was talk of peelers slaughtered and pitched battles with the military. Whatever the truth, one thing was certain: there'd be trouble tonight.

At the Harp and Shamrock a deep thunder menaced the air. The revellers fell silent. No one moved. It grew louder. Now it could be clearly heard: the crashing of boots on cobbles. The drinkers on the pavement scattered. There was a surge from the bar to the door.

'Feckin' peelers!' Those in the doorway elbowed their way through the crush, flapping like men trying to take flight. Glasses hit the flags and the beer exploded.

The evening of the rescue, Wednesday 18 September, the police descended on Angel Meadow, Hulme and Chorlton-on-Medlock, the Irish areas of the city, rounding up everyone who fell into their hands and hauling them off to Stanley Street police station. Head Constable William Palin rushed back to the city and took control of the investigation, and when he arrived witnesses were already identifying the men who filled the corridors and holding cells.

Palin's handsome face had already assumed the pained mask of rage and humiliation it was to wear for many months. His thick, neat moustache, clear complexion and brisk manner made him the quintessential Indian army officer. Though recently appointed and on leave at the time of the rescue he knew that he would carry the blame for the catastrophe. In broad daylight in the centre of one of Britain's greatest cities a bunch of savages had assaulted a body of police officers, slaughtered one of them, wounded others and secured the release of the most dangerous men in the Empire. It had happened on his watch and Palin took the outrage as a personal affront.

Under his unruffled exterior Palin was a stew of humiliation. He was not simply the bluff military auto-maton, blinkered to everything except his role in the administrative machine. He was perceptive and sensitive to slights and he was fully aware that the institution for which he was answerable had failed to discharge its responsibility. He had failed.

Palin did not need *The Times* to tell him the significance of his failure. Nevertheless, its editorial declaimed, 'The Fenians have declared war against our institutions and have carried it into the very heart of the country.'

He had served the Empire and was a committed advocate of its mission, which was to enlighten those fortunate enough to fall under its benevolent sway. Christianity, progress, education, culture – in short, civilisation – was its bequest. There were, of course, those who, because of ignorance, superstition, the cant of priests, their lower nature or their susceptibility to troublemakers, resisted this blessing and even regarded it as an imposition. So much the worse for them. They must never be allowed to wreck a sacred mission and to impose their chaos on the world.

What piqued Palin even more than his own sense of failure was the general atmosphere of blame as all concerned sought to divest themselves of responsibility. Political opponents and some elements of the press sought to attribute the disaster to the government's generally irresolute attitude to the Fenian threat. Sensitive to these charges, Prime Minister Derby and Home Secretary Gathorne-Hardy deflected blame onto the Manchester authorities.

Rumours that the Manchester police had failed to respond to at least one and possibly two telegrams warning of the Fenian plans further undermined the credibility of the force. One version circulating in the days immediately after the rescue was that no one had thought to open a warning telegram from Dublin until after the event.

In trying to save face, Palin at first denied the existence of any telegram telling of the rescue plan. This stance soon became untenable and on 12 October the papers published a revised account in which Palin claimed that the telegram advising a strong guard on the prisoners had arrived at 2.15 p.m. on 18 September. Eight extra police were assigned because of this information and the prisoners were handcuffed while in transit as an extra precaution. This telegram, Palin claimed, came from Dublin and no mention was made of any other warning communication.

This version of events was confirmed by the findings of the watch committee, the organ of local government responsible for policing Manchester, which found that a junior clerk, William Mellor, received the Dublin telegram at 2.05 p.m. on the day of the rescue. It was addressed to Detective Maybury, who was not in the office at the time. Mellor opened it and passed it on to Inspector Garner at 2.15. Garner sought out Maybury, but could not find him. Instead he met Superintendent Gee near the city courts and warned him of the telegram's contents. The detectives then arranged to strengthen the escort.

The disaster which followed, however, required a scapegoat. Inexplicably, the committee resolved that 'William Mellor, the junior clerk in the detective office, be dismissed from the service on the grounds of incompetency.' Shortly afterwards Maybury – who like Mellor was blameless – threw himself on the sword of 'retirement due to ill health'.

However, this did nothing to sate the demand for vengeance against those responsible for the rescue. The enormous demonstrations demanding an extension of the franchise, which had recently choked London's thoroughfares, and lurid revelations of intimidation, violence and murder as tools of trade union power, reinforced the feeling among the public that the established order was under threat. Daily the newspapers reported instances which seemed to prove that the tentacles of the Fenian conspiracy extended into every corner of the country and threatened to destroy the peace and security of the entire nation.

Fenians detonated a bomb at Woolwich Arsenal; they

shot two policemen in London; they were plotting to murder Middlesbrough's local elite; they were within a few minutes of blowing up gasworks in both Manchester and Liverpool; armouries all over the country were liable to raids; they were drilling on moors and hillsides in every part of the country; they were planning to slaughter hundreds of innocent people, including women and children, by derailing trains; and they even sent men to Balmoral, no doubt as part of a plan to murder Queen Victoria. No sooner had the newspapers assured the public that the guard at the royal residence had been reinforced than it was regaling its readers with details of a Fenian plot to assassinate the prime minister, Lord Derby, and his home secretary, Gathorne-Hardy.

Little wonder that thirty-five authorities, abandoning England's boast that the British police could maintain law and order without recourse to armed officers, acquired weapons for their constabulary. Public disquiet reached such a pitch that the government even considered suspending habeas corpus, as it had in Ireland after the rising of March that year. The Fenian John Devoy later summed it up perfectly in his memoirs: 'Nothing had ever occurred in England to create such a wild panic.'

Palin knew that the only way to reduce his ignominy was to capture all those responsible. The government, however, was not prepared to leave the matter in Palin's hands and sent its top men to oversee the operation.

Williams, Campbell and Clarke were Scotland Yard's

experts on the Fenians. Between them they'd spent years lolling around railway stations, scrutinising the faces alighting from the Holyhead boat train. They were the men who cultivated the new arrivals who'd fallen on hard times and gave them a few shillings a week. All they had to do in return was keep the Yard informed about what was going on – a new face, or perhaps an old face missing, rumours and gossip. The three were avid readers of *The Nation*, *The Freeman's Journal* and *The Irishman*. They travelled regularly to Dublin to liaise with their colleagues in G Division of the Dublin Metropolitan Police. Now they were despatched to Manchester to organise the hunt.

Between the rescue and the trial of those arrested in its aftermath nothing was heard in Manchester except the diabolical plots and murderous plans of the Fenians. Local papers were full of it, faithfully reproducing stories culled from newspapers as far away as Australia. The Fenians were the talk of every alehouse, the sole topic of conversation in every shop and marketplace where loyal citizens gathered.

Even before the men from Scotland Yard reached Manchester, a number of Fenians, taken at the scene of the attack, were crammed four to a cell in Stanley Street. By nightfall on the day of the rescue, fourteen had been arrested. Later another nine joined them. During that night they lined the corridor, some in chains, while a succession of witnesses stared into their frightened eyes. One prisoner had a white handkerchief around his head.

Though there was no sign of Kelly or Deasy, the police

assured the public that they had made significant captures. As *The Manchester Courier* of Friday 20 September told its readers, among those arrested were William Allen and Michael Larkin. Both were charged with murder, 'Allen having been positively identified as the man who shot Brett' and Larkin having been 'seen to assist in overpowering Brett and to put him in such a position that Allen could shoot him'. As far as the newspapers were concerned, there was no doubt about it: the murderers were already in police hands. But certain sections of the public believed Larkin and Allen weren't the only ones who deserved to twitch at the end of a rope.

Some of the workers at Taylor and Son, a Barnsley linen mill, knew that Fenians were everywhere. As loyal subjects of the queen, they took action. Among their fellow workers was an Irishman. His workmates needed no further evidence against him than his nationality. Nevertheless, they held a trial at which he was duly sentenced to death and then they threw a rope over a beam in the warehouse and strung him up, his legs flailing. Some less patriotic workers saved him. But every day further revelations were tightening the noose around the necks of those in custody.

The Manchester Courier of 21 September was certain that Allen and Larkin were guilty of nothing less than the cold-blooded murder of Brett. It told its readers that when the van arrived at Albert Street police station it was found that 'there is no sign of any bullet having been fired through the keyhole, and the presumption is that the fatal shot must have been deliberately fired at Brett through the wicket ventilator, which had been forced open. The assassin would have a full view of Sergeant Brett.'

As news of the arrests spread, crowds gathered around the police station in Albert Street. They filled the road, passing the time in banter with a detachment of the 57th Regiment of Foot who lined the footpath around the station and guarded the rear and side doors. When a police van parted the bodies, discordant hissing filled the air. The soldiers strained against the mob. Prisoners blinked in the light as they emerged from the Black Maria and recoiled from the lurching faces, some baring their teeth and spitting venom. One spectator's tongue lolled on his chin, his eyes rolling in his skull as he yanked on an imaginary rope around his neck.

The gentlemen of the press were also out in force. Nothing in the appearance of the prisoners surprised them. Most were clearly 'the lowest class of Irish', though, surprisingly, some looked like 'respectable artisans'. Most had been taken with no more than the usual resistance, certainly nothing worthy of note. It wasn't until the Friday after the rescue that the police encountered their first major problem.

On that evening, 20 September, the police swooped on 68 Buckley Street, Rochdale Road, in Irish Town, where they expected to find the Sherry brothers, James and John, known for their Fenian sympathies. The police caught the men unawares and bundled them into the van without a struggle. Their house guest, John Nugent, the man who had evaded the police when they had arrested Edward Condon, however, proved to be an entirely different proposition.

He was a powerfully built man of six foot two inches, who, according to the press, 'took part in the Fenian rising in Ireland'. Though the house was surrounded when the police broke in, Nugent escaped into the yard through an upstairs window and hid in the outside water closet. When discovered he refused to surrender and, armed with a saw, managed to keep the police at bay for fifteen minutes, before they overpowered him. Conveniently, when the police searched him they found a letter congratulating him on his recent escape from the grasp of the Irish authorities. Subsequently, Constables Yarwood and Trueman – the latter had travelled in the cab behind the Black Maria – identified him as one of those most active in the Hyde Road rescue.

In Manchester on the Saturday night and Sunday morning after the rescue the police arrested another nine men and dragged them to Albert Street station. Early on Sunday morning they seized a further four, including John Bacon, the keeper of a beer house on Cable Street, identified as the lame man with a stick who had been seen inciting others to attack the van.

Having apparently arrested everyone in Manchester who might have been involved in the rescue – and many others who couldn't possibly have been – the police extended their trawl to include not only Manchester's outlying towns but also Liverpool and the area within the city's orbit. Daily news of new captures provided further proof of the pervasive menace of Fenianism.

James Woods, a twenty-two-year-old Irishman, was arrested in Ashton-under-Lyne and brought to Manchester where he was identified as a participant in the rescue. On 1 October *The Manchester Courier* reported that Liverpool police had arrested a man suspected of involvement in the rescue.

Days after this the newspapers reported that Fenians had attempted to fire Chester police station, causing only slight damage. No one was arrested and no evidence was cited to suggest that Fenians were responsible, yet such was the media obsession with the enemy within that it was assumed that they must be. It was *The Manchester Guardian* which best expressed the fear that gripped the country:

> It is apparent that we are in the presence of a very active and extensive conspiracy, the members of which will shrink from no crime ... to promote their objects. A similar hidden agency is at work in most of the large towns. In Manchester there exists a formidable organisation for the purpose of ... war against the state. The plot is really a conflict with society at large. If authority is to be assailed in this manner, nothing holds together.

It was clearly the duty of the government to make an

example of the Fenians – even, the newspaper suggested, if this meant that some innocent people might be punished.

Further driving this clamour for decisive action against the Fenians was the public sympathy aroused by Brett's fate. His death incensed the public to an extent hard to imagine today. At the inquest, in the presence of Brett's inconsolable wife and daughters, Constable Shaw, who had ridden on top of the Black Maria, named the killer. He positively identified Allen as the man who shot both Brett and Sprosson, the civilian wounded in the foot. He told the coroner he'd seen Allen fire and then heard, from inside the van, 'He's killed'. Immediately after that, the door was opened and Brett's lifeless body fell out.

At this stage of the inquest the clerk displayed Brett's helmet. Congealed blood surrounded the hole the gunshot had punched through front and back. When asked to identify the helmet Constable Shaw broke down and wept. The coroner heard that his police colleagues had taken Brett to the Manchester Royal Infirmary but that he never regained consciousness and took to his grave the secret of the identity of the man who fired the fatal shot.

The evidence presented at the inquest boded ill for the prisoners, providing further revelations suggesting that the Fenians had set out to murder Brett and anyone else who stood in their way and that the outcome of any subsequent trial was a foregone conclusion.

The inquest elevated Brett to the status of a Victorian hero. The public appetite for the details of his life was insatiable and for several weeks newspapers published whatever snippets of information, no matter how inconsequential, they were able to gather. Many readers contributed anecdotes about his family and his military and police career. A clear picture emerges which served to reinforce public affection and make him a real victim, a man easy to identify with and not merely an impersonal official.

Charles Brett was an unlikely hero. Certainly, he was a decent, compassionate family man, but his working life was made up of mundane tasks. A sergeant in the Manchester police force, attached to the court in Bridge Street, he passed his days in the company of petty thieves, beggars and prostitutes. He was well known throughout the city, seen every day the court was in session sitting atop the Black Maria in which he conveyed his charges.

In his private life he was a loving family man, a caring husband and father and a loyal son. One of four brothers who all served in the army, he joined the Manchester force in 1846 and became a sergeant in 1852. After six years on the beat he was transferred to court service, a role for which he was ideally suited. At fifty-one years of age, he was known as a good neighbour and a man who lived an exemplary life. He and his family were regular attendees at St Barnabas', Oldham Road, his local parish church.

A former soldier, like many nineteenth-century peelers, Charles Brett had served the Manchester force for twenty-one years. His wife was fifty-four and they cared for the sergeant's elderly father. His was the model, respectable working-class family: his eldest daughter Mary, twenty-three, was a factory hand, his son Charles, twenty-one, a soldier in the Grenadier Guards and his younger daughter, Elizabeth, eighteen, had attained the position coveted by all aspiring working-class girls – an assistant in a draper's shop at six shillings a week.

Yet unremarkable as all this was, Charles Brett became a quintessential Victorian role model, a humane and courageous man with a powerful sense of responsibility. When threatened with a pistol and ordered to hand over the keys, he refused, saying, 'I'll do my duty to the last.' Several witnesses testified to his words. No one could have produced a better epitaph or more eloquently expressed the dilemma he confronted with such fortitude. It was this, rather than the fact that he was the first Manchester police officer killed in the exercise of his duty, that won him public acclaim.

The inquest aroused great sympathy but it was his funeral that confirmed Brett's status as a model of courage and dedication to duty. He was buried on a Saturday afternoon and in the words of *The Manchester Courier*, the public demonstrated 'intense interest' in the funeral. Fifty thousand people lined the route. Manchester and Salford dignitaries attended, including the mayors, both chief constables and other leading police officers, together with a large contingent of both police forces. The rector of St Barnabas', the Brett family's own parish, officiated.

The funeral of Sergeant Brett
Courtesy of Mercier Archives

A cortège over a quarter of a mile long snaked into Harpurhey Cemetery. Never before had there been such a display of sympathy for a man who was not a public figure. Few of those present doubted that he was a victim of the brutality and anarchy which the Fenians embodied. In honouring him the Manchester public were proclaiming their hatred of those responsible for his death and asserting their determination to oppose them with the same resolve that cost Brett his life.

Brett's position between exemplar and symbol is neatly encapsulated in a phrase from his memorial card. It baldly states that he was murdered by Fenians and concludes:

Ye who think yourselves much stronger,
Ye may be the next to fall.

Is this no more than Victorian mawkishness in acknowledging that death may strike at any time? Or is it a reference to the pervasive Fenian threat?

The extent to which the case captured the public imagination is shown by their generosity. Over £600 was raised by donations. This was mainly in pennies and halfpennies from factory workers whose wages were from fifteen shillings (seventy-five pence) to £1 per week. In addition the police watch committee awarded Mrs Brett a pension of twenty-one shillings a week for her life and a sum of £300 paid to her children on her death.

Nor was interest in Brett confined to Manchester. All the major national newspapers covered his funeral. *The Times* ran a detailed account which captured the reaction of the family: 'Brett's relatives yesterday were almost overwhelmed by the magnitude of the popular demonstration in his honour. Considered as a public funeral, the multitudes who attended it rendered it one of the most imposing ever witnessed.'

Brett's funeral made the Fenian threat real in a way that nothing else had and increased the public appetite for information about their dastardly intrigues. The popular press reported every rumour uncritically, seldom seeking evidence for what often turned out to be nothing more than hearsay. All the Manchester newspapers reprinted in their entirety Fenian stories published elsewhere, the cumulative effect of which was to create among all social classes a sense of a pervasive danger.

On 7 October newspapers reported that the victim of an attack in Holborn, London, the bandsman Edwin McDonnell, had died. There was no information on McDonnell's background or why he was shot. The Holborn police, however, had no doubt who was to blame and arrested an Irishman, John Groves, believed to be part of a Fenian 'shooting circle' – a band of trained assassins – who they thought had mistaken the unfortunate bandsman for the notorious spy John Joseph Corydon.

McDonnell's funeral, with full military pomp, at Windsor Cemetery, attracted considerable media interest. The whole regiment and the bands of the 1st and 2nd Life Guards, with the Royal Horse Guard following, turned out. Groves' trial, however, raised many concerns about the nature of the judicial system that would soon determine the fate of the men taken at Manchester. The police persisted in prosecuting Groves although the victim failed to identify him before he died and an expert witness, a gunsmith, testified that the gun found in Groves' lodgings was not the murder weapon. What's more, it came to light that a key prosecution witness, a cabman, was in fact a serial witness, always ready to oblige when a police case suffered from an inconvenient lack of evidence. Another witness vital to the prosecution case turned out to be a convicted perjurer.

Proceedings became farcical when a prosecution witness stated categorically that the assassin was bearded. Groves was clean-shaven and had never had a beard. Undaunted, the police produced a number of barbers in an attempt to demonstrate that Groves might well have been wearing a false beard on the night of the murder.

Eventually the prosecution dropped the murder charge, though they won a conviction on a lesser charge which resulted in Groves serving five years' penal servitude. Though he had escaped the gallows, the case boded ill for any man brought before a court charged with Fenian activity.

On 8 October the home secretary instructed the chief commissioner of the metropolitan police to ensure that escorts carrying cutlasses guarded all prisoners in transit. There was to be no repetition of the errors that had made the Hyde Road rescue possible. The public were assured that the authorities were constantly vigilant and prepared for every eventuality. They needed to be, for, as the papers never tired of telling their readers, the Fenians were relentless in their efforts to undermine law and order and no one was safe from them, not even law-abiding citizens who were in daily contact with the police. This became apparent when a police witness who had identified a

Fenian suspect complained to the magistrates' court that James and Mary Foley had threatened him, warning him of the dire consequences of giving evidence against their countrymen. The two were quickly imprisoned.

Meanwhile the debate which had sprung up about holding a special commission was settled. From the day of the rescue, there were those who maintained that swift and decisive justice could not be achieved through the normal courts. To wait for the regular winter assizes, they said, was foolish and dangerous. It would encourage the Fenians to commit further atrocities by giving the impression of a weak and dithering government. What was needed, they said, was a special court that would deal out swift justice and a clear warning.

Those who opposed the idea of a special commission, such as Manchester's Councillor Thompson, argued against trying the case in 'hot haste and hot blood'. Injustice, resentment and even greater bitterness were likely to be the outcome, he explained to a hostile council chamber. The crimes had to be 'viewed in a political context' and a period of time allowed to elapse to avoid a trial in an atmosphere in which, according to one nationalist newspaper, it was impossible for the men to get a fair trial as 'every Irish Catholic was regarded as a Fenian and every Fenian an assassin'.

The government decided. The case was to be tried by special commission.

Councillor Thompson was not the only member of

the Manchester City Council to oppose the commission. Councillor Booth also feared its consequences. The majority of the city's Irish population, he said, in no way supported the outrage. Over the previous thirty-five years, he had seen a gradual absorption of the Irish into the community as they had become more law-abiding and happy with British institutions.

But Booth's and Thompson's words of sweet reason found no resonance in the wider community or even within the council, which backed the government's decision. The advocates of moderation found themselves in a dwindling minority as the authorities' resolve continued to harden. *The Times* accurately expressed government thinking when, in an article that mentioned Allen by name, it said, 'one execution now may save the necessity for many executions later'.

The people of Manchester were certainly in no mood for restraint. *The Irish Times* for 25 September reported that 'an unreasonable spirit of hostility and distrust has arisen against all Irish artisans in Manchester'. Attacks occurred daily. John Devoy later spoke of Irishmen being beaten up and fired from their work. The *Daily Telegraph* spoke of the 'alien colonies' that Ireland had planted in the northern towns and said they were hotbeds of 'the fiercest treason'. It demanded punishment that 'must be quick as well as stern'.

The Manchester Courier did nothing to calm the situation. On 27 September it carried a report that reads like blatant anti-Fenian propaganda. A meeting of Fenians in Sunderland, it claimed, had passed a resolution 'expressing their joy at the murder of Sergeant Brett'. No source was quoted.

Every day there was the steady drip of reports of Fenian activity, the effect of which was to convince the population that the peace and security of the nation and the safety of every law-abiding citizen were threatened. Each outrage was more blatant than the last.

Events in Ireland also heightened tensions and exacerbated communal strife. News of the Kelly and Deasy escape sparked wild displays of delight. Crowds gathered in many cities and towns to taunt peelers and soldiers and in Limerick the provocation proved too much for the 74th Regiment, who bayoneted several civilians, killing one. On the Friday after the rescue there were ongoing clashes between the police and military and the civilian population of the city. The whole police force was on duty in an attempt to prevent a further clash.

The funeral of William Kelly also heightened tensions. He was one of the many interned under the Suspension of Habeas Corpus Act, part of the government's response to the 1867 rising, which allowed arrest and imprisonment without trial. His time in the Limerick County Gaol broke his health and soon after his release he died. Thousands stood at his graveside, mourning another victim of British brutality and contempt for justice.

All the talk of Fenian activity clearly unnerved the

Manchester authorities. The City Council demanded an investigation into the arrangements for those arrested in connection with the Hyde Road rescue and lodged in the New Bailey Prison, Salford, and was assured that they were beyond any rescue attempt. The prison had been made impregnable. It seems the police, afflicted by foreboding, were trying to assure themselves that they were ready for any eventuality.

The Irish Times, generally a good guide to government thinking on Ireland, reported that 'something is brewing for another outbreak far more formidable and determined than the last'. Any area with an Irish community was suspect. Bacup, a small Lancashire town fifteen miles from Manchester, was such a place. It was hardly surprising, therefore, that the police should receive reports of Fenians drilling there.

Liverpool, long a Fenian stronghold, attracted intense police activity from the middle of October onwards. Earlier in the month troops had moved into the city. The newspapers reported that since the death of Brett a number of prominent Fenians had surfaced there and the police closed in, hoping to make a spectacular catch.

Their attention focused on an alehouse at 25 Adlington Street, purportedly the centre of Fenian activity in the city. A large body of police, led by the head constable of Liverpool, surrounded it. A strong back-up force, no doubt expecting that the locals might try to impede arrests, supported them. Adlington Street, according to the papers, was in an area 'chiefly occupied by the lowest class of Irish', where hostility to the police was a powerful sentiment. On this occasion the resentment was confined to cries of derision and expressions of sympathy for the arrested. Ultimately, however, the police were disappointed. They tried to justify their ostentatious show of strength by claiming they had made significant arrests, but it was clear that once more they had acted on faulty intelligence.

Four of those arrested, including James Chambers, said to be Liverpool's head centre, were brought to Manchester under armed guard on suspicion of involvement in the Manchester rescue. The other three were Joseph Brophy, Patrick McDonough and John O'Brien (alias Lanigan). When they appeared in court, they were described by the press as having 'the appearance of the lowest class of Irish'. McDonough and Lanigan were so insignificant that no evidence was presented against them and they were discharged.

Of all those arrested, fifty were eventually charged with complicity in the rescue and of these, thirty were committed for trial. None of the witnesses to the rescue put the number of Fenians involved at more than twenty.

On 27 October a special meeting of the Manchester justices, held to prepare for the forthcoming trial, agreed a resolution which 'render[ed] every citizen whose name appear[ed] on the city roll liable to be sworn in as a special constable'. If necessary, every loyal citizen was to be enlisted as a soldier in the struggle against the Fenian terror.

How did the Manchester Irish feel about all this? Mrs Patrick Scully, the wife of a fish hawker, best expresses their attitude. The Scullys did not live in an Irish ghetto and paid the price. Malicious neighbours reported Mr Scully to the police and he was taken away in a van. As the van rumbled out of the street, his wife ran after it and shouted to the gawking neighbours: 'Thank God he's not taken for stealing but for that of which any Irishman ought to be proud.'

Scully's wife faced down the authorities with defiance and courage. But proud of her husband as she was, she knew Patrick was no more than a minor figure momentarily caught up in something not of his making. For others, however, the Hyde Road incident proved the defining event of their lives.

6

'HOT HASTE AND HOT BLOOD'

Wide-eyed, their mouths ajar, the children in the crowd lining the route said not a word. The jangling of the horses' bridles, the slap of scabbards on sleek horseflesh, the hollow ring of the metal shoes on the setts played the symphony of a great army on the march.

Never before had Manchester prisoners had such an escort – Hussars in scarlet tunics, the light glinting on the blades of their naked sabres, the cold grey of the rifles and the prison vans with their roofs crowded with peelers. Somewhere, in the midst of this great cavalcade, with armed men before and after them, to their right and their left and above them, rammed so tight in the Black Marias that each could feel the man against him breathing, were the prisoners. Though it was a cold day, sweat made their flesh tacky.

In addition to the escort, another 2,000 troops stood ready in the surrounding towns with many more on standby in Liverpool on that Saturday, 27 September. Among those gathered outside the court were plain-clothes detectives, specialists in countering Fenianism, from Dublin, Liverpool and London, on the lookout for known conspirators. Others sat in the public gallery. Police at the entrance searched everyone.

Just as intimidating as the escort was Manchester's assize court to which the prisoners were taken for the preliminary hearing. No building in the city was better able to impress the accused with the power and majesty of British justice. Its three great neo-Gothic entrance arches were as overwhelming as those of any medieval cathedral and its elaborate magnitude spoke of fearsome power. Though new, it seemed to suck up from the ages a timeless permanence. The geometrical designs of the tracery on its enormous arched windows did not tell of the Scourging at the Pillar or the Crucifixion but nevertheless spoke of a power beyond the simply human, an authority in excess of anything wielded by mere men.

On that unusually bright September morning the light from the twelve-foot windows illuminated the stark mahogany interior of the criminal court. The enormous chamber dwarfed those about to play out their assigned roles. Its single adornment was the legend placed beneath the principal gallery and facing the witness box: Thou shalt not bear false witness against thy neighbour.

A full bench of magistrates, led by the stipendiary magistrate, Mr Robinson Fowler, were seated with several army officers in full uniform. Before them stood the five charged with the murder of Sergeant Brett: Michael Larkin, William Allen, Michael O'Brien – known by the alias William Gould throughout the trial – Edward Condon – known as Edward Shore – and another man called Thomas Maguire, a royal marine. Another twenty-four were charged with lesser offences in connection with the rescue. All wore handcuffs. They sat on two benches facing counsel, and suspended above the head of each, for ease of reference, was a number.

***

In the days immediately before the trial the public attitude to the men had hardened. *The Spectator* summed up prevailing sentiments when it spoke of the 'incomprehensible patriotism of the Irish' and demanded 'quick and severe punishment' on the grounds that any delay would cause 'the English mob to take the law into their own hands'. The *Saturday Review* and the *Observer* agreed that the outrage was the result of the government's misguided clemency in dealing with the perpetrators of the rising of March 1867. This grave mistake, the *Review* added, must not be repeated.

It appeared that the press was united in an effort to undermine every possible extenuating circumstance surrounding the death of Sergeant Brett. *The Morning Herald* spoke of the Fenians' 'imaginary grievances' and castigated the late government for its lenient policy, particularly its early release of Fenians sentenced to long periods of imprisonment. It called for the government to 'strike terror into the hearts of evil-doers'. *The Manchester Courier* assured its readers that an examination of the Black Maria uncovered nothing to support the suggestion that whoever shot Brett did so inadvertently while trying to shoot off the lock. The *Courier* was adamant on this point: whoever shot Brett did so deliberately and with the intention of killing him.

***

If the national attitude was hardening, so too was local sentiment. The *Daily Telegraph* reported on the day of the magistrates' hearing that 'The people of Manchester have not concealed their detestation of the deed', a cryptic reference to the daily attacks on Irishmen. The *Telegraph* repeated a view which was now becoming commonplace, speaking of the 'alien colonies' that Ireland had planted in the northern towns and assuring its readers that they were hotbeds of 'the fiercest treason'. Ominously it called for punishment 'quick as well as stern'.

The *Manchester Weekly Times* stressed the need to strike at the enemy within. The raid on the van, it claimed, revealed the extent of that 'mad movement in our midst'. Nor should anyone be surprised, it continued, that this movement had sympathisers in a city which was home to so many 'ignorant and uneducated Irish'. To confirm its low opinion of Fenians, the paper then went on to list the defendants together with the employment and educational status of each. Most were 'imperfectly educated' or had 'no education' and were employed in unskilled manual jobs.

Curiously *The Irish Times* of 25 September was one of the few national journals to demur at the prevailing mood, reporting that 'an unreasonable spirit of hostility and distrust has arisen against all Irish artisans in Manchester'. This hostility was not confined to the city's slums. It was reported on 27 September that five men who went to the court to provide an alibi for some of the prisoners were themselves identified as participants in the attack and taken into custody. Clearly anyone prepared to give evidence in favour of the accused risked arrest and prosecution.

This made the task of Ernest Jones and William Prowting Roberts, the pillars of the defence team, even harder. Both men were acutely aware that the mood in the city was bound to work against their clients and sought from the beginning to have the case moved away from Manchester. This was not an unusual request. In previous years the infamous mass murderer, William Palmer, was tried at the Old Bailey when his defence successfully argued that his local infamy was such that he could not get a fair trial in his home town of Stafford.

Jones and Roberts also sought a deferment, not only to allow passions to cool, but more significantly to give them time to interview their clients and prepare their defence. The government, however, was adamant: the trial would go ahead immediately and would take place in Manchester.

This decision, made before the court heard any evidence, was a serious blow to the defence case and though both men made little of it to their clients, they realised its dire significance. Many commentators believed that the atmosphere in Manchester was so inflamed that it was impossible for the men to get a fair trial there.

Jones and Roberts, however, remained obdurately positive. They themselves were one of the few reasons for optimism among the accused, as in them they had advocates of experience and commitment who were in sympathy with their political aims. Both were widely known for their support, over many years, of democratic and nationalist causes. Both Chartists, their interest in Irish independence was not merely professional. They had urged those campaigning for universal suffrage to put their weight behind the campaign of the Irish Confederation, an association established by the Young Ireland movement to work for Irish national independence. Their stand on this and other issues suggests that they had considerable sympathy for those who took up arms in the cause of Irish independence.

Ernest Jones had been editor of the Chartism movement's newspaper and was a man who had suffered imprisonment for his political beliefs. In 1848 he had been sentenced to two years' solitary imprisonment for making seditious utterances. In prison, though forbidden writing materials, he wrote a poem, 'The New World', a statement of his political aspirations, in his own blood using a quill made from a feather he picked up in the exercise yard, inscribed on the blank pages of his Bible. Though Jones was fond of the kudos of victimhood and liked to exaggerate the extent to which he had suffered for his political ideals, there is no doubt that he had suffered.

By the time of the trial Jones was a man of comfortable proportions with a nose like the beak of a toucan, a receding hairline and sad eyes. His demure exterior belied his fervour in the courtroom.

William Prowting Roberts was also a Chartist of the 1840s who suffered imprisonment for his activities. He was involved in a series of Chartist trials, including that of the movement's leader, Fergus O'Connor. He was solicitor to Marx and Engels, a close personal friend of Mazzini, the Italian nationalist leader, and a pamphleteer, orator and publisher. He regarded himself as a class warrior and was best known as a full-time trade union lawyer who gloried in the title of 'The Miners' Attorney-General', having acted in many cases on behalf of girls and women working in the mines. He was never known to turn away clients because they could not pay.

Both Jones and Roberts were publicly vilified for their work on behalf of men widely regarded as national enemies and, during the trial, both received death threats. Nor did those admitted to the public gallery hide their disdain: at every opportunity they hissed and booed both men.

As the trial was about to begin Jones looked tired and drawn. He huddled with Roberts and continually pulled

The trial of the Manchester Martyrs
Courtesy of Mercier Archives

at his toucan's nose as if he would shape the tip to a point.

The prosecutor, W. H. Higgin, deputy recorder of Manchester, stood to speak, turning his eager, fleshy face up to the magistrates. It was the face of a child anxious to please, his jowls and bright eyes giving him the disarming appearance of a chipmunk. He spoke with great deliberation, like a man certain of the facts who is not used to being challenged.

'The nub of the case,' Higgin said, 'is that Sergeant Brett was threatened that if he did not give up the keys he would be shot. When he refused,' he paused, 'Allen fired a shot – with deliberate aim. One of the women prisoners in the passageway, on threat of being shot, handed up the keys.' He stopped and turned a page of his notes. Looking at the prisoners he said, 'Allen and Larkin played a prominent part throughout the attack on the van. But that is irrelevant.' He raised his head and looked at the bench. 'The law is perfectly clear. All involved in the incident are equally guilty of wilful murder.'

Higgin sat down. Yarwood, one of the peelers who had ridden atop the Black Maria, was the first witness up. In a monotone, he claimed that O'Brien shot the horses and Larkin fired at him (Yarwood) three times.

When questioned, he admitted he did not see anything in Allen's hand, although he insisted he did see Michael McGuire (one of those charged with lesser offences), standing on the embankment near the bridge. He gave the impression of a man trying to answer honestly.

Jones, meanwhile, seemed more and more agitated. Pulling his nose he whispered feverishly to Roberts. Looking from side to side, his forehead creased, frowning through his half-moon glasses at first the prisoners and then the magistrates, he sprang to his feet. 'This is the first time in an English court that prisoners have been brought before a preliminary hearing in handcuffs,' he said. Jones' manner was indignant, like that of a man appealing to a fundamental principle of decency so obvious that he is affronted at having to defend it. Immediately those in the public gallery started up a menacing hissing.

'The manacles worn by the prisoners are causing the men considerable suffering,' he declaimed. 'The nuisance they cause is not only an indignity, unworthy of a civilised country, but is preventing the men attending to the proceedings.

'Further,' he added, his voice rising in contention with the hissing from the public gallery, 'I protest at the unseemliness of the magistrates sharing the bench with members of the military.'

'The military,' Stipendiary Magistrate Fowler said, 'have been brought in by the authorities, who believe certain precautions necessary. However, if any prisoner is suffering I will order larger handcuffs.'

The colour rose in Jones' face. 'As a member of the bar I decline to sit in any court where the police are allowed to override the magistrates, or lend myself to such a violation of the course of justice.'

The hissing started again, louder than ever.

Jones turned to Roberts. 'There is your brief, sir, I am sorry to have to return it.' He handed Roberts the brief and, heels thundering on the tiles, marched from the court, his gown flapping around his hips. The hissing from the gallery coarsened to jeering.

'I request an adjournment until the handcuffs are removed,' Roberts said.

Fowler replied, 'I cannot grant *that*,' his teeth biting off the last word.

'It's cowardice and nothing else,' Roberts said. 'The men here are as quiet as sheep in a pen. It is monstrous to keep them handcuffed during the inquiry.'

Fowler looked shaken by this bombardment. 'I will ask the magistrates to adjourn with me and we will consult Captain Palin. No one will be more willing than I to have the men unshackled.'

Roberts shouted to the door of the court, 'Ask Mr Jones to stop – we may have something like justice at last.' The hissing started again and the peelers led the prisoners down to the cells.

Back in the court twenty minutes later Fowler spoke to the defence. 'We are unanimous in our decision. Under the circumstances, the handcuffs cannot be removed.'

Cries of 'Hear, hear' filled the court and Fowler rapped his gavel with a sound like a distant Gatling gun. 'I warn you now,' he called, his voice cracking with annoyance, 'if there is any further expression of feeling I will clear the court.'

He then turned to the dock. 'Since Mr Jones has left the court, your solicitor Mr Roberts will no doubt watch your case.'

'We placed our liberties and lives in the hands of Mr Jones and if this court think it proper to take one or the other by foul means, let them take it,' replied O'Brien.

Fowler shook his head. 'You decline to be defended. That is all we have to do with it.'

'I decline to be defended unless Mr Jones defends me,' said Condon.

'You shall have every opportunity to cross-examine witnesses yourselves,' said Fowler.

'I shall take no further part in this,' said O'Brien. 'It is a farce so far as I am concerned.'

'Very well,' said Fowler. 'Proceed.'

Now the events took on a life of their own. Like the slick vaudeville shows O'Brien and Condon had seen in New York, one witness followed another in dizzying succession. The performers knew their roles and it was as if Higgin, like a suave compère, prompted each to play them to the full.

Patterson, a passer-by, clumped to the stand. He was a squat, gruff man, who chewed his words and spoke into his muffler. When Fowler asked him to speak up, he gave him the slow stare of a debt collector.

'Allen was on top of the van,' he said, 'trying to break through the roof. [Thomas] Maguire there was throwing stones up to him.' He spoke without looking towards the dock. 'As Kelly escaped from the van, I heard Allen say, "Kelly, I'll die for you before I'll give you up".'

Then a brick maker, Pickup, appeared. Shorter than Patterson, he was far broader. In a piping whine of a voice he said he saw Larkin trying to break into the van with a hammer. Allen, he said, fired through the ventilator about six times. He heard him say, 'Kelly, didn't I tell you I'd die for you? I'd lose the last drop of my blood for you!' He also said that John Gleeson and Patrick Coffey – two of those charged with lesser offences – were there throwing stones.

Mr J. Cottingham, who together with Jones and Roberts, was acting for the accused, raised his long, weary body and spoke for Gleeson, telling the court that Pickup was the only witness to claim that he was there. Gleeson's employer, he added, swore that the man was at his work with the Yorkshire and Lancashire Railway Company on the day of the rescue. Fowler discharged Gleeson. Two turnkeys unfastened his shackles and led him from the dock. Around his broad mouth was an incredulous smile.

Next came Griffiths, a hairdresser, whose shop was a few hundred yards from the bridge. He was a man of middling size with pale skin and sloped shoulders. He spoke clearly. 'I saw Allen shoot at Shaw and Trueman and then shoot Sprosson in the leg.' Later he claimed he saw Allen shoot into the back of the van and would not be shaken on this. 'I saw Allen fire again shortly after, as I thought, at the lock of the van.' Michael McGuire, he said, was one of those who attacked the van.

A young street urchin, George Mulholland, who had been playing near the bridge when the van was attacked, picked out Thomas Maguire as one of the men on top of the van. 'Allen there fired through the ventilator. Sergeant Brett was inside holding the ventilator shut and when he fired through someone called out, "He is killed, he is killed".'

John Beck, a railway porter, in a black jacket worn shiny with age and with enormous drooping pockets, took the stand next. He pointed out Michael McGuire, Larkin and O'Brien.

'I saw Allen shoot through the ventilator and then shoot Sprosson in the foot,' he said.

'How is it that all these people say they can identify me, when I'm as innocent as the child unborn?' There was a silence before people realised it was Allen who spoke. Every head in the place turned to him.

Fowler looked up from his writing, staring over the half moons of his glasses. 'Any remarks about these proceedings must be left to your legal advisers,' he said.

Constable Trueman, his hands and feet appearing too big for his body, his face tired and his voice slow, said he saw Condon there. 'I saw Allen fire into the van and heard a woman's voice call, "He is shot".'

Elizabeth Robinson, who was walking along Hyde Road when the Black Maria was attacked, said she saw O'Brien with a revolver.

A barman, George Meyer, contradicted the other witnesses. According to him, Larkin shot Sprosson. Henry Slack then said he was driving his cab up behind the one with the peelers following the prison van. He was certain that it was Thomas Maguire who was on top of the van trying to break through with a stone.

William Hughes, the next witness, disagreed. Maguire, he said, was the one who was handing up the stones to someone else who was on top of the van. According to him, Larkin ran in front of the horses to stop them.

Next Higgin rose, his well-scrubbed face bright with sweet reason. 'The identification of McWilliams,' he said, 'is doubtful.' The prisoners looked back at McWilliams – he was at the end of the back bench. His head bowed, he did not respond to the mention of his name. He'd always maintained that the police had snatched him off Rochdale Road on the day he arrived from Australia. Higgin told the court he would offer no evidence against the man. Fowler ordered his release and the turnkeys again shuffled sideways between the benches towards him. Unaware of what was happening they had to raise him from the bench by his elbows. He went with them with no more enthusiasm than if they were taking him to his death.

Fowler ended the session. Everyone stood. Some of the men tried to rise from the bench but were yanked back by the chains that tethered them to their neighbours. The turnkeys eyed them with the slow malice of the powerful. The magistrates and the military snaked from the bench.

The prisoners shuffled to the stairs that dropped steeply down to the cells, shambling like old men, their jarring little steps like the walk of the palsied. Once in the corridor to the yard they were lined up, two by two. O'Brien was tethered to Allen, who had the unfocused eyes of a man whose attention is locked inward, so intensely preoccupied that the world of the senses barely registers. It had certainly been a bad day for him as witness after witness spoke of his prominent role in the rescue, testified that he had a gun and told of him firing into the van.

In subsequent days the accused heard the same story many times. It was as if they were stuck in a quagmire which sucked at their legs, drawing them down to inescapable suffocation.

***

That night, as for several nights in the early stages of the trial, none of the principal defendants slept more than a few fitful hours. They lay in the chill darkness reliving the events of the day, endlessly reviewing what had been said and weighing the credibility lent to it by the inflections and demeanour of the speaker. No matter how much they gnawed at it, no matter how often they turned it over in their minds and viewed it first from one angle and then from another, it always amounted to the same thing: there was nothing to hearten them.

The next day they were back in court, still manacled.

Roberts immediately complained to Fowler that the police were tutoring the witnesses to identify prisoners by their position in the dock and asked that they change position. Fowler agreed.

The turnkeys pushed and steered the men like bewildered cattle.

Almost immediately Fowler announced that there was a case against Allen, Condon, Larkin, Maguire and O'Brien.

Shortly after this the court discharged the Martin brothers, William and John, as the sequence of events that had brought them to court became clear. A few hours after the rescue, William Martin's sister-in-law sent him with a message to a house near St Philip's Park. Unsure of the way, he stopped at Park Gate to get his bearings. Unfortunately for Martin, Inspector Gill chanced along and seeing him flushed and suspicious, grabbed him and took him to the police station, chained him to O'Brien and then presented him to a drove of witnesses, eight of whom duly swore to seeing him take part in the rescue.

When William Martin told his story the police arrested his brother, John, and repeated the process that led to William's identification, with the same result. At court, Beck, one of those who had identified William Martin, got hopelessly confused when questioned by Roberts: he couldn't remember which brother he had seen taking part in the rescue. Fowler discharged William and the prosecution decided not to proceed against John.

The story of the Martin brothers highlights the concerns expressed by the *Law Times*, which was seeking new guidelines for judges to ensure that convictions were no longer based entirely on eye-witness identification. Such identifications were problematic as it was customary for the police to repeatedly summon witnesses to the station to have them identify the accused. There is no doubt that the police often jogged reluctant memories and pointed out specific individuals they suspected of criminal activity.

What's more, there was nothing to prevent witnesses from discussing the matter. In this case, where most of them lived in a small area near the bridge on Hyde Road, it is certain that their role in the trial was a constant topic of conversation which bestowed on them both kudos and local celebrity. How tempting to exaggerate one's involvement and to increase one's importance by assuming an unjustified confidence in identifying suspects!

This danger was particularly acute in this case because many of the potential witnesses, including all those in the Black Maria, were petty criminals who might reasonably expect a degree of official indulgence in return for helping the police. There was also the possibility of a share of the reward money on offer and the fact that the police were under enormous pressure to ensure a conviction. As the trial of John Groves, the man accused of the murder of the Holborn bandsman, had demonstrated, there were a number of people always ready to oblige the police by swearing to events as and when required to secure a conviction. Given the strength of anti-Fenian hostility in the city there was certainly reason and opportunity for the police to resort to such measures. Indeed, during the trial *Reynold's News* decried what it called 'the infamous system of police tutorship' exposed by the 'identical evidence of several eyewitnesses'.

After the Martin brothers left the courtroom, the next witness, Emma Halliday, appeared. She was one of the prisoners locked inside the van with Kelly and Deasy. She proved more convincing than those brought against the Martin brothers and spoke deliberately and with confidence.

'Charlie opened the ventilator to see what was going on.' She threw her head back as if delivering a song.

'What did Sergeant Brett say when he looked out through the ventilator?'

'"God bless my soul",' he said, '"it's them Fenians." He pressed down with his hands on the ventilator to keep it closed.' Then she said, looking up at the public gallery, 'Someone shouted into the van, "Give out them keys." But Charlie said he wouldn't.'

'What happened then?'

'What happened then?' She laughed, shaking the hair from her shoulders. 'Why, everyone knows what happened then. The same voice came through the ventilator.' She stooped and cupped her hand in front of her mouth. Now her voice was a whisper. '"Give up them keys," he said, "and we'll do you no harm."'

'And what was Sergeant Brett's response?'

Now she straightened herself and once more tilted her chin to the gallery. She spoke in a declamatory voice. 'Charlie said, "No. No, I'll do my duty to the last."'

She stopped. Higgin allowed the silence to intensify. At last he spoke. 'What then?'

'They forced open the ventilator – Charlie couldn't hold it closed – and wedged it open with a stone. I knew they was going to shoot Charlie so I pulled him away from the door. His head came on line with the ventilator and one of them fired a shot.' She paused. 'I saw the man what fired the shot,' she said, turning to Fowler.

'Stand up,' said Fowler, looking at the accused.

'That's him,' she said, pointing at Allen. 'It's him what killed Sergeant Brett.'

She also identified Michael McGuire as being present at the attack, claiming that having fled the Black Maria she ran towards the gaol and, looking back, saw him throwing stones.

Next came Ellen Cooper, an older woman, also one of the prisoners standing in the passage with Halliday. She was the one who had handed out the keys after Brett was shot. She told the same story as Halliday and also pointed out Allen as the man who spoke through the ventilator and threatened to blow her brains out if she didn't give up the keys. She claimed that she also saw Michael McGuire throwing stones.

Again, Higgin was on his feet, his face sleek with benevolence. The witnesses due to speak against the Sherry brothers, Bryan, Morris and Daley are not reliable, he said. No evidence will be offered against them. Again, Fowler ordered their release. The turnkeys entered the dock and separated them from their partners. They showed no emotion but allowed themselves to be led out.

That evening Allen swaggered from the dock, glaring up at the public gallery, his shoulders pushed back like a fighter taunting the crowd. But once in the van, his shoulders collapsed. He slid to the floor and his head dropped to his knees.

Whatever hope Allen and the other principal defendants

had nurtured was crushed early the following day by Elizabeth Robinson. Neither a prisoner nor a streetwalker she was different from the other women. Everything about her spoke of respectability – her bell-shaped dress of blue shot silk with a velvet trim and a narrow white collar; the way her hair was done in a chignon, worn inside a net, supporting a dark pork pie hat. She moved like a lady on smooth, invisible steps. Higgin's manner was oilier than usual. When Robinson spoke, the magistrates listened with something approaching awe. Fowler for once left off his writing and raised his head to look at her.

It was not what she said. The women in the van had given more damning testimony. It was her voice. She didn't speak with the language and cadences of the whores and drunkards. She spoke like Fowler and Higgin, like Roberts and Jones. Her voice was slow and clear.

She said only two things: she saw Allen with two re-volvers and she saw O'Brien by the van. The defence asked her no questions.

The court next addressed the matter of the picturesque fantasist John Francis McAuliffe. Offering a single piece of evidence – that a policeman had seen him shake hands with a woman who had brought Kelly and Deasy their breakfast – the prosecution claimed he was an accomplice of the Fenian leaders. However, Fowler refused to refer him for trial based on that evidence alone. Once more McAuliffe had inveigled himself into events which were not his concern. Like those habitual confessors who claim to be guilty of every high-profile murder, he was a man desperate to be at the centre of great events, though destined to be always on the periphery.

For those who were at the centre, the situation continued to deteriorate. Constable William Carrington was the next to identify Allen.

'Point out the man you saw,' said Higgin. Before Carrington could respond, Allen spoke out: 'It's me he means.'

The crowd hissed.

'That's him, all right,' said the peeler.

Next came Walton, a wall-eyed tobacconist whose shop squatted between two others near the arch.

'I saw Allen fire two shots through the ventilator on two separate occasions. The second time, I heard a cry from inside the van. A woman called out, "Charlie is shot."'

'Be so good as to point out this man,' said Higgin.

'Oh, he knows me well enough,' said Allen, 'you have no occasion to ask him.'

Walton continued, 'I heard him say, "Kelly, I told you I would die for you rather than give you up", as he released the Fenian leader.'

Higgin consulted his notes.

As if impatient to give his evidence, Walton continued, 'I also saw Gould, Maguire, Shore, Larkin, Nugent ...'

''Tis by the names he's going!' cried Larkin and Nugent, protesting at Walton reeling off this list.

Fowler hammered his gavel until the court fell silent. The questioning continued.

'Why did you offer yourself to the police, Mr Walton?' Roberts asked.

'Because I am a patriotic Englishman, determined to oppose the Fenians.'

'Did you say in court that you would hang all Fenians?'

'Not in court,' said Walton.

'When did you express it?'

'When Larkin was captured in the railway yard. I told him that I had never seen a man hanged yet but, if you are hanged I will come and see you.'

Walton was revelling in his celebrity, smirking at the public gallery and undermining the solemnity of the situation. Fowler sought to stop his antics.

'You are making an exhibition of yourself now.'

'You mean to go and see him hanged?' asked Roberts.

'I will, sir, if I live.'

Again the magistrate tried to bring an end to Walton's mockery of the proceedings: 'Won't you, Mr Roberts, allow this exhibition to pass by?' asked Fowler.

Roberts looked at Fowler, then at Walton with disgust. 'I have done,' said Roberts, dropping into his seat and shaking his head.

Once more Higgin turned his unctuous smile on Fowler. He did not, he said, intend to offer evidence against Patrick Kelly. Kelly had always maintained that he had arrived from Leitrim in search of work just the day before the rescue.

One of the peelers, Taylor, who had been riding on the

van, said he saw Allen firing at anyone who approached it. He identified Nugent and Hugh Foley as having guns and Bacon as the man with the crutch who had cheered on the attack on the Black Maria.

'Is it correct, sir, that you failed to identify any of those named at the police station immediately after their arrest?' asked Roberts.

'That is correct, sir,' answered Taylor.

The prosecution was now down to the dregs, those who wanted the authorities to overlook a theft or ignore a street brawl. They would side with their sworn foes, the peelers, against a common enemy and so earn a little leeway. Or perhaps they hoped for the approval of their neighbours by playing their part in hanging a Fenian.

First of these was Hunter, a labourer, who sprang into the witness box and smiled all round him like a man about to sing a comic song. He told Higgin the usual story: he had seen Allen fire into the van.

'Did you not say that all Fenians should be hanged?' asked Roberts.

'I said I would hang Allen for what I saw him do,' replied Hunter, still grinning.

'And what makes you grin?' Roberts asked. 'You are a bad 'un.'

'Now, Mr Roberts, I think he has given his evidence very fairly and you have no reason to say that,' warned Fowler.

'I don't think he has,' retorted Roberts. 'I know he has lied about the hanging and I shall express my opinion.'

The mob hissed, Fowler hammered and Hunter turned his malevolent smirk on the accused.

Within a few minutes they had run through the remaining witnesses. Richard Bromley and Joseph Smith both swore they saw Allen with a gun in each hand. Kate Reilly, who had been on her way to scrounge money from the prison chaplain, said she had seen Allen, Miles Brennan and Thomas Maguire at the rescue.

Spencer, a travelling hawker, said Allen was holding a gun, and also identified Larkin and O'Brien.

Yet again Higgin rose and turned his smile on Fowler. Addressing the bench, he said that the commanding officer of one of the accused, the marine, Hugh Foley, had given him a good character reference and none of the witnesses had identified him. Higgin would, therefore, offer no evidence against him. Once more the turnkeys came into the dock. There was plenty of room now and Foley rose to meet them, his face gaunt and his eyes beseeching. As they unlocked him, his chains jangled.

There was less room in the dock the next day. Six other prisoners, taken in Liverpool, were brought up with those who had been there since the beginning of the trial.

Roberts squeezed fistfuls of his gown as he rose to his feet. He asked Fowler for more time to prepare his case. 'I will most decidedly throw up my briefs rather than stand here professing to represent men whom I have not seen for an hour – the whole lot of them.'

The hissing began again.

Three of the new men were remanded for the next day. The rest – Nugent, Lynch and Moore – were discharged for lack of evidence.

The final witness was Heely, a gas meter inspector. A shy man who spoke to the ground, he squirmed as he answered. He saw the shot fired into the van but had not seen the man who fired it since. Higgin asked him to look at the men in the dock. Reluctantly, Heely raised his head and made a slow sweep of the faces.

'No,' he said. 'He's not there.'

The following day, the defence began its summing up.

'The outrage of which these men stand accused has created a mob hatred against all of the lower class of Irish,' said Roberts. 'Yet their intention was never to commit murder. They assembled not to rescue ordinary criminals, but to rescue two men not convicted, but accused of, a political crime. Their crime too is political.'

'The evidence against these men is seriously flawed. The people in the best position to identify those who took part, and the people who make the best and most reliable witnesses, have not been called. Only six of the twelve policemen there have been called and they have identified only four people. The policemen, Shaw and Knox, who were there throughout the whole episode, identified no one and the same applies to Mr Slack, the omnibus proprietor.

'Many of the witnesses were in court when other witnesses were giving their evidence. All the witnesses pointed out that the death of Brett was unintentional and stated that many who were there were in no way involved in the attack.

'Thirty-five innocent men have been arrested and discharged because there is no evidence against them. How many more are still in custody?

'In cases such as this there are always those who are anxious to help the police by testifying to what they have read in the newspapers. It is not hard for the police to "get up" any number of such witnesses, always anxious to be of assistance by swearing away the life of an innocent man. Walton is such a person. As for the prostitutes and felons who came here in the hope of a share of the reward money, their evidence is totally worthless.'

Roberts then called up the defence witnesses, each appearing at great risk. The police had already arrested and charged four men who had come to the court for this purpose.

Roberts told the court that many of the accused could prove their innocence. Eight men gave Thomas Johnson an alibi. One was the timekeeper and the rest his workmates. John Brannon had seven witnesses who put him on Rochdale Road at the time of the attack and Patrick Kelly from Galway – not to be confused with the Leitrim man of the same name, already released – had five witnesses who put him at his work in Oldham Road potato market. Six of Thomas Ryan's fellow workers testified he was at his job all day. A number of workmates testified for Michael McGuire, Thomas Kennedy, William Murphy and John Neary. Ten people swore for the joiner John Francis Nugent, six for Michael McGuire, four for Charles Moorhouse and John Carroll and three each for Henry Wilson and Timothy John Featherstone.

'William Gould,' interjected Fowler, addressing Michael O'Brien, 'have you any witnesses to call?'

O'Brien looked around and then, relenting his previous decision to take no part in proceedings, answered: 'I am confident justice cannot be done here.'

Fowler looked affronted but O'Brien carried on.

'I wish to call the persons who tore my clothes at Belle Vue, the parties who chained my hands and feet and left them on all night while I was identified ...'

'Desist from these observations! This court has already shown you more consideration than many others might. Do you have any witnesses to call?'

'Do you expect a prisoner who has been locked up in his cell all day to give you the names of police officers?' O'Brien said.

'Proceed then, Mr Roberts,' Fowler answered.

Roberts brought up Mary O'Leary. She and her brother-in-law, Henry Wilson, one of the accused, together with his wife and youngster, had gone to Belle Vue gardens on the day of the attack. O'Brien, relenting of his decision to offer no defence, tried to establish that when the van arrived at the arch he was in the Justice Birch opposite the gates of Belle Vue Prison.

'Did you see me there?' O'Brien asked.

'You came in and spoke. A cab passed while I was speaking to you,' she answered.

'Do you remember what I was doing at the time – was I playing with a child?'

'Yes.'

'And a policeman was striking the outside of the cab with his hands as though he was drunk or excited?'

'Yes, I remember that well,' she answered.

'That man was Yarwood,' said O'Brien, turning to the bench. 'Didn't I part from you and walk in the direction of Manchester?'

'Yes.'

'I wish to call Yarwood,' O'Brien said.

Yarwood took the stand.

'Were you the officer who went to the gaol for assistance?' O'Brien asked.

'Yes,' Yarwood replied.

'Was your head not out of the window and were you not striking the outside of the cab with your hands?'

'No. I had my head out of the window but I was not striking the outside of the cab.'

'The driver of that cab will prove it. Will you swear you did not see two men, a woman and a child near the gaol gates?'

'I did not see them.'

'Did you see anyone on the sidewalk?'

'No.'

'It's a lie and you know it.'

'You must behave yourself, Gould,' called Fowler.

Next came Drysdale, the inspector in charge of the Albert Road station. His uniform was brushed clean and he stood erect in the witness box, clearly experienced at giving evidence in court.

'What was I wearing when I was brought to the station on the night of the raid?' O'Brien asked.

'You were wearing leg irons and handcuffs,' the inspector replied.

'What was I wearing when the witnesses were asked to identify me?'

'You were still wearing the leg irons and handcuffs.'

'And would this have given the impression to those asked to identify me that I am more dangerous and must have committed some greater crime than the others in custody?'

'It would.'

'I was treated with indignities that were not heaped upon anyone else. I was made to wear prison clothes. Spies and pimps were put to looking at a hole in the cell door to see if they could identify me. If I had not been an American citizen no such thing would have been done. I am an American citizen and I am proud of it.'

The only response to O'Brien's complaints was hissing from the gallery. Fowler fixed O'Brien with his narrow stare. Then he remanded twenty-three of the accused to the New Bailey to await trial.

Writing of the events surrounding the rescue years later

in his memoirs, John Devoy, the Fenian memoirist, claims that of the twenty-three men remanded, only four had taken part in the rescue.

That afternoon the van carrying the prisoners turned towards Salford, instead of making its way to Belle Vue as it had since the beginning of the preliminary hearing. Entombed though the prisoners were, the reek of the Irwell penetrated the van as they crossed the bridge linking Manchester and Salford. Old people called it the 'bridge of sorrow'.

The van drove through the prison gates. The stench of the river slapped them in the face as they stepped down into the yard, their limbs stiff from the long hours they been sitting in the cold courtroom. The damp cobbles glistened.

The turnkeys led them past the treadmill, into the building, a column of palsied men, their chains chattering. The prison was a cavern reeking of human waste. Warders bawled in a sing-song details of the prisoners to the turnkeys. The slap of their feet on the flags bounced around the walls.

That night, Jones brought news of Brett's inquest. The verdict was wilful murder against Allen and others unknown.

7

'MY BLOOD WILL RISE'

His long arm snaked out from his body and a bony finger, the same parchment hue as his face, stuck out from his scarlet gown. He stabbed it in the direction of William Prowting Roberts.

'Take that man into custody and remove him!'

A peeler moved towards Roberts as Digby Seymour raised his hand and advanced towards the scowling judge. As Roberts looked about in dismay, Seymour's soothing tones mollified Mr Justice Blackburn. 'Mr Roberts,' Seymour explained, 'is hard of hearing, Your Honour, and did not understand your instruction that he should desist from objecting to those proposed for the grand jury.' Seymour begged the judge's further indulgence. Blackburn relented and Roberts was allowed to remain.

The defence team – Roberts, Jones, Seymour, Sergeant O'Brien and Cottingham – knew that several major battles they had fought already in the magistrates' court had to be reopened before the commission. These related to three things: the trial venue, the composition of the jury and the validity of the warrant under which Kelly and Deasy had been held. The lives of the accused might well depend on the outcome of these issues.

From the first day of the hearing before the magistrates' court the defence had maintained that any trial held in Manchester was bound to be unfair. The authorities had imposed a complete lock-down and the city resembled territory occupied by an invading army. The 72nd Highlanders and a detachment of Hussars, bristling with bayonets and sabres, atop and all around the prison van, continued to set the tone for each day when they conveyed the accused from the New Bailey Prison in Salford to the assize court. With them was Captain Sylvester, the head constable of Salford, in charge of a large force of armed policemen, and M. L. Trafford, the stipendiary magistrate for the Salford Hundred, at hand to authorise force against civilians by reading the Riot Act.

Peelers lined the route and in all the adjoining streets, mingled with the regular police, were auxiliaries, mainly sturdy men in bulky topcoats, 'Special Constable' emblazoned in scarlet letters on their white armbands.

The hostile atmosphere in the city had intensified in the days before the commission opened. *Reynold's News* described the city as in the grip 'of anti-Irish hysteria'. The defence request for a change of location cited the 'extraordinary precautions' as one factor likely to prejudice any trial. Additionally, it pointed out, there were the exaggerated fears and rumours of a Fenian rising in the area from which the jurors were drawn, the attitude of the local press, the demonstrations of hostility during the magistrate's hearing and the fact that it was too soon after the events to prevent the hysteria it had generated from influencing the trial.

The government, however, had not sent a special commission to Manchester to have it refer the matter to a court in London. Mr Justice Blackburn – who together with Mr Justice Mellor presided over the commission – would have none of it, as one might expect of a man whose characteristic sympathy for the accused is suggested by his sobriquet, 'the hanging judge'. John Mellor had a fixed, cold stare and though at fifty-eight he was older than Colin Blackburn, he looked younger. The government had chosen Blackburn and Mellor because they were regarded as two safe pairs of hands.

The importance the government attached to the case is demonstrated by the choice of the attorney-general, Sir John B. Kerslake, to lead the prosecution, assisted by two queen's counsels, Percival Pickering and Robert Scarr Sowler. Clearly, Lord Derby and Gathorne-Hardy were leaving nothing to chance.

Having failed to get the trial moved, the next task the defence faced was the selection of jurors. They objected to every one who lived in the Manchester area but Roberts, either because he was hard of hearing or because of excessive zeal on his clients' behalf, continued to object to jurors even after Blackburn had warned him that counsel alone could make objections. It was at this stage that the judge ordered Roberts' arrest, then was persuaded by Seymour to relent.

The third issue, the status of the warrants on which Kelly and Deasy were held, was the most significant of the three as the defence maintained that this was such that a charge of murder against the defendants was invalid. The defence argued that the whole nature of the case was entirely different if Kelly and Deasy had been held illegally. They maintained that both men were held on remand without any evidence being offered on the charges stated in the warrant and that therefore the charge against the rescuers should be reduced to manslaughter. The defence believed they had found at least one relevant precedent, comparable in every respect.

The court rejected this and Blackburn again stated that if there had been a common design to rescue the prisoners by the use of violence, if necessary, the charge was one of murder. Yet it is clear the issue of the warrant, which the defence broached on many occasions, raised a number of key concerns.

The case opened with the first batch of men, the 'principal defendants' as they were known – Allen, Larkin, O'Brien (Gould), Condon (Shore) and Thomas Maguire – answering to the charge of wilful murder. Eighteen others stood accused of lesser, though still serious, crimes in connection with the rescue.

The court and the conservative press even now refused to

acknowledge the political nature of their crime. They were to be treated like common criminals, like thieves who had conspired to rob and murder for material gain. The national press had no doubt as to the outcome of the trial. As *The Times* told its readers, 'the legal position is clear: all those who took part in the affray are equally guilty of murder. The trial will be short and will satisfy the universal demand for the speedy punishment and death of the leaders.'

The prosecution put up fifty-seven witnesses who had already been examined and another twenty-five not yet examined. The defence subpoenaed over one hundred witnesses. This was necessary as many of the defence witnesses had taken fright, not simply because anything which suggested sympathy for the Fenians was likely to incur retribution by their neighbours and workmates, but because witnesses for the defence knew they ran the risk of being arrested and charged with involvement in the rescue.

Events outside Manchester, which had nothing to do with the Fenians, further contributed to the heated atmosphere surrounding the trial. It seemed to many that the established order was under attack from all sides. Gargantuan crowds were massing in Hyde Park in support of the Reform Bill which would extend the right to vote to those outside the traditional propertied classes, who many regarded as the country's natural leaders. Who could tell what mayhem they might unleash? The royal commission on trade unions had uncovered evidence that there were many prepared to murder anyone who prevented them from manipulating working men for their own subversive ends. Was it possible that anarchists and communists had wormed their way into working-class organisations and were perverting them into instruments of revolution? It seemed that every week gave rise to a new threat to the lives and security of the British people, rich and poor alike.

At the same time the malign ambitions of the Fenians apparently knew no bounds. Informants reported rumours of plots to assassinate not only the prime minister, Lord Derby, and his home secretary, Gathorne-Hardy, but also the queen. The authorities drafted in soldiers to guard Balmoral and the cabinet debated suspending habeas corpus in Britain as they had in Ireland.

The mood in Manchester was growing increasingly hostile. Trade was slack: the manufactories and warehouses spewed workers out onto the streets. Restless, they drifted about the city looking for diversion. The fund-raising events organised to pay for the Fenian prisoners' defence aroused hostility and several suffered from violent attacks. In the nearby town of Wigan, a mob attacked and destroyed Irish homes. The atmosphere around the assize court on the bleak October day the commission began its work was equally intimidating. When the van arrived, the crowd surged towards it and began hissing and hooting, as if baiting a bear or barracking a fighting cock.

The soldiers shuffled into their customary formation, a phalanx between which they steered the prisoners to the doors of the court through the shrieks of abuse.

Once inside they were propelled along the corridors, where all the windows were barricaded against a Fenian attack, put in the cells and had their manacles removed. Peelers then filed them up the steep steps to the dock where Thomas Maguire, solid and squat, stood apart from the others – the diminutive Larkin, the smiling O'Brien with the posture of a soldier, the rangy Allen and the assured Condon. All bore the marks of confinement: the dank cells had sucked the colour from their skin, and Larkin's eyes seemed pushed back into his skull.

Blackburn's skin was bloodless too. But his was the colour of old parchment. His words were measured, cold and relentless.

He addressed the court: 'The principal crime you have to inquire into is the death of the policeman, Brett.' Blackburn bent forward, the ball of his left hand clasped in the fingers of his right. The eyes in his desiccated face looked down at the papers on his desk. Occasionally they flickered over the lenses of his spectacles, as his head twitched slightly, like that of a watchful bird. 'There was only one shot fired and only one man could have fired that shot.' His high shoulders held rigid, he moved in his chair, turning slightly towards the jury.

'However, whenever persons agree amongst each other to take part in an unlawful action, every person involved in such an action is equally guilty of murder – if that crime is committed – as the person who fires the fatal shot.'

If so, the defence team asked themselves, why are all the

rest not also tried for murder? Why only the five? No one broached this issue as it was clear that in Blackburn's view this inconsistency would best be resolved by charging *all* the men involved with murder.

As if reading their thoughts, Blackburn pursed his dry lips and continued, 'Everyone who was present aiding and assisting is equally guilty of the crime of murder as the one who fired the shot.' Again he paused. 'It follows,' he said, 'that anyone whose actions show that he was there to help the escape – especially the possession of firearms – is guilty of murder.' His eyes flickered once more over the half-moon lenses. 'The only difficulty you will have is as to the number of prisoners.'

Kerslake stood, tall and erect, his back as stiff as a coffin lid. He had a large head, whiskers and a chin like Punch's. His enormous chin tilted back, he began by outlining the prosecution case with a frightening fluency and coherence. All those who took part in the rescue, he explained, certainly knew that dangerous weapons were to be used; they knew what was to be done and consented to it and therefore were quite prepared to kill anyone who interfered with them. He spoke of the importance of this case as a warning to others, showing them that the country's laws were strong enough to protect Her Majesty's subjects and society from such an outrage. Then the procession of prosecution witnesses began again.

Peeler Shaw again said that he was near the door of the van when the shot was fired and he identified Allen as the gunman. 'I saw him put his pistol to the door of the van, either at the keyhole or the air hole a little above it but I think it was the keyhole.' Later he added, 'My impression was that Allen fired to blow off the lock.'

'I did not get a clear view of Maguire's face,' said Shaw, 'but I believe he was the man with a white hat who assisted with breaking into the van.'

Under cross-examination, Frances Armstrong, one of the prisoners who had been standing in the corridor of the van, had to admit to a string of convictions for drunkenness and theft.

'Him what asked for the keys had a small moustache,' she said. 'That's him,' she said, pointing at the smiling and clean-shaven face of William Allen. 'Anyways, it's very like him. I'm almost sure.'

Jones then rose to address the court on the matter of the warrant. He spoke with great urgency and conviction.

'The whole nature of the case is entirely different if Kelly and Deasy were held illegally. In fact, they were held on remand without any evidence being offered on the charges and therefore the charge against the rescuers should be reduced to manslaughter.'

He then questioned Inspector Garner: 'And where, sir, is the warrant on which Kelly and Deasy were first remanded?'

Inspector Garner was clearly agitated. 'It no longer exists,' he replied, his voice barely audible. Jones prolonged the silence.

'How is that, sir?' Jones' tone was that of someone enquiring of a friend about his health.

'I destroyed it, sir.'

'Destroyed it? Is it your practice to destroy warrants?'

'No, sir.'

'Pray tell the court, Inspector Garner, how many warrants you have destroyed in the course of your career as a police officer.'

'Only one, sir. Just this one.'

Blackburn looked down on the proceedings with cold displeasure. He spoke through his dry lips.

'It is for the jury to decide if the prisoners had a common design to use violence in rescuing Kelly and Deasy. If so, the court believes the crime would be murder – regardless of the status of the warrant on which the prisoners in the van were held.

'However,' he continued, addressing Jones, 'I am prepared to allow you to submit further cases of precedent to the court.'

The parade of prosecution witnesses continued and prompted by Kerslake's nodding chin, each told his story. They spoke with flat vowels and harsh, clipped phrases, as if they would bite off the words as they escaped from their mouths. To the ears of the accused it was if they spoke a language different from that of the legal men. The witnesses studiously avoided looking at the accused as if they shunned the sight of them, fearful of the look of men they would condemn to death.

They all told the same story: Allen shot Brett, Larkin fired into the van and O'Brien shot one of the peelers, while Maguire and Condon took a leading part in the rescue. Over and over they repeated it in a hundred different ways, until it acquired a certain validity, like a story repeated down the generations. At last it ended.

Roberts rose to speak. He began to meticulously dismantle all that had gone before. He penetrated the oppressive burden of testimony and light passed through it, revealing inconsistencies, highlighting doubts and uncertainties, exposing lies.

He showed that the idea that Thomas Maguire was there was pure fantasy. His sister testified that he lived with her in Preston Court, Greengate, Salford. The house is two miles from the site of the attack on Hyde Road. She swore he was in the house all day. 'It was his custom to lie in bed when he was on furlough. He didn't get up until about 3.30 p.m.'

'I spoke to him through the window of my house,' said Mary Egan, a neighbour. 'It was between 3.30 and 4.00 p.m. He was in Mrs Parkins' – his sister's – yard. He asked if he could go to the party with me.'

'I saw him washing himself in the yard at 4.30 that afternoon,' said Martha Handcock, another neighbour.

A third neighbour, Louisa Carroll, saw Maguire in his sister's house. 'That was between 3.30 and 4.00 p.m.' She was not the only one. James Grant, another of Maguire's next-door neighbours, saw him in his house just before four o'clock. Elizabeth Blackburn, a widow who lived opposite Maguire, saw him at the same time.

'I saw him cross the yard to the closet at about four o'clock and again at six o'clock,' said Mrs Ingham, another neighbour.

Then came all those who swore to Maguire's character. It was clear he was a man who'd spent his life in the British navy and had no interest in politics. He was one of those men whose life was composed entirely of things that touched him personally. His world consisted of his relations, friends and workmates and all his concerns related to them. Politics was an incomprehensible realm which did not impinge on him. He left that kind of thing to others and was as likely to enter into a political discussion as he was to venture an opinion on Aristotle's *Poetics*.

Next the defence tried to establish that when the attack on the van began O'Brien had not been at the arch but some distance away outside the Justice Birch, the pub directly opposite the entrance to Belle Vue prison. A young lady, who had lost her position as a governess because she had given evidence on behalf of O'Brien at the magistrates' court, nevertheless appeared again.

She was strong and composed. Kerslake was oily and wheedling, his tone overly polite, coaxing and considerate.

'O'Brien was at the door of the Justice Birch, opposite Belle Vue. It was just before four o'clock,' she said.

Kerslake probed and pressed, trying to catch her off balance, his great chin nodding. But she never faltered, remaining assured.

Others said they'd seen O'Brien at the door of the Justice Birch at ten minutes to four. Then the peeler, Gee, admitted they'd kept O'Brien chained hand and foot when they brought in witnesses to identify him.

Then it was over. The last witness was gone. All that remained now was the summing up.

And the verdict.

***

That night, as the accused went back to the New Bailey, they knew that the uncertainty was about to end. For some, anything was better than living their lives in abeyance. A grim acceptance settled on them. They had little confidence in a judicial system that had so often meted out destitution and death to their countrymen. Yet the uncertainty still tortured them and hope worried away at their resignation.

***

The next morning Roberts rose to speak for the defence for the last time. His manner was slow and measured, his round face and stubby hands working in unison with his deep voice. As they listened, the men's spirits rose.

What he said was so reasonable. It was obvious Maguire was not there. There was no proof that either Larkin or O'Brien had revolvers. Allen wasn't the man who shot Brett. Roberts made it clear that there was no evidence against him.

'This case has taken place at a time when a panic prevails throughout the country, making it impossible to view these events in a dispassionate way. You must disregard the hysteria and confine yourself to the facts.' He stressed the last word with a gesture of his right hand like a man firing a shot from an imaginary revolver, flicking his squat index and forefinger at the jury.

'There has been talk of hundreds of shots being fired. So why was only one revolver – a single weapon – produced during the course of the trial? If their intent was that of murderous desperados, why is it that not one witness claims they used violence to protect themselves from capture?' He paused, as if waiting for a reply. When none came, he proceeded.

'Maguire is a man with thirteen years' unblemished service in the Royal Marines. You have heard the testimonials as to his good character and listened to the witnesses who place him miles away at the time of the crime. He is as likely to be a Fenian as is Mr Justice Blackburn. He is here today only because of a tragic case of mistaken identity.'

'Remember,' he said, skewering the air with his forefinger, 'those who were not aware of the intent to use dangerous weapons cannot be guilty of murder. There is no evidence that any of the accused deliberately injured anyone. Let me remind you what Constable Shaw said: "My impression was that Allen fired to break the lock of the van".'

'And what of the witnesses?' Roberts paused to let the question resonate.

'Of some, I say nothing. They themselves have already said enough to allow you to form a true opinion of their veracity. They are of those thoughtless people who are always ready to support the police by swearing to a man they have seen but once. The case of William Martin shows the evil consequences of this false testimony.'

Again Roberts paused. He cast his eye over the jurors.

'One thing that suggests the testimony against Allen is very weak and suspect is that the events took place in the middle of great confusion. Let us compare it with something that took place at the start of the incident and before all the witnesses – the shooting of the horses. Between them they would have us believe that three different people shot the horses. Yarwood has told us that Larkin shot the horses. Yet at the magistrate's court he claimed that Larkin caught the horses by the bridle. Shaw, from the same vantage point as Yarwood, failed to corroborate his evidence. George Mulholland told the magistrates it was Allen but now he tells us it was Larkin. Knowles says O'Brien fired at the horses. William Hughes says he saw Larkin running before the horses but says nothing about his shooting them. Detective Taylor, sitting at the front of the van with an excellent view, says nothing about either Larkin or Allen. If they cannot agree on this matter, why should we accept their testimony on other matters?'

Once more he seemed to be waiting for the jurors to reply.

'Someone climbed up on the van and in full view of all the witnesses spent some considerable time trying to break through the roof with stones which had been passed up to him. Who was on the roof and who passed up the stones? According to Patterson, it was Allen who was on top of the van and Maguire who handed up the stones. No, says Mulholland, it was Maguire who was on top of the van. Not so, says Pickup: neither the man on the top of the van nor the stone passer is in the dock. And Knowles agrees with him.

'What of those best qualified and most experienced in the giving of evidence, those practised in accurate observation and the faithful recounting of events – the police officers who were at the scene of the crime? Why were all not called? When they were called, their evidence undermined the prosecution case. Though witnesses claimed O'Brien, brandishing a gun, pursued Constable Trueman, Trueman himself did not say that. Indeed, he did not identify O'Brien.

'The charge of murder is totally ridiculous. It would have been far more plausible to have charged them with high treason. But to do so would have been to admit that their rescue was a military action and a political act.

'I beg you remember, gentlemen, this one thing: we have established that Allen may not be the man who shot Brett. In law "may not" means "was not".' He emphasised this with a stroke of his hand – a chopping movement.

Roberts sat down.

Blackburn's dry lips moved. 'Your task, gentlemen of the jury, is simple. Murder is killing with malice aforethought. Murder in law is not confined to cases where this intention is to kill a specific person. If a shot is fired to disable a man so as to carry out a plan and that man is killed, then that is murder. If the rescuers planned to use violence to carry out the plan if necessary, then they are all equally guilty.' The shrivelled skin of his face moved as if it would crack. Beneath his wig he looked like a decrepit rake whose decomposing flesh was dusted in powder. Periodically his body twitched.

'There is reason to believe,' he said, 'that Brett was shot deliberately.'

With that he sent the jury away to consider its verdict. O'Brien noticed that the light – what could be seen of it from the barricaded windows – was fading fast. Darkness was closing in on the court. It was ten minutes after six o'clock when they brought the prisoners down.

When they brought the prisoners back up the clock showed twenty-five minutes past seven. The darkness now made a perfect mirror of the windows. The only sound was the hiss of the great gas mantles, suspended from the ceiling. The light wavered as someone opened a door behind the jury box. Then all in court lifted their heads at the noise of feet on the tiles. First a rumble, then a crisp clatter, tapering to a shuffle as the jurors entered their benches and then the self-conscious tapping of the last juror's feet. Then silence.

The prisoners had their eyes raised to the ceiling, all except Maguire, who looked directly at the jury. Condon lowered his eyes and, seeing the foreman with a piece of paper in his hand, fixed him with a reproachful stare. Allen's expression was that of an intransigent schoolboy who is about to be soundly thrashed. 'Do your worst!' it said. 'You can't hurt me.'

The clerk rose. 'Gentlemen of the jury, have you agreed upon your verdict?'

'We have.'

'Do you find William O'Mara Allen guilty or not guilty of murder?'

'Guilty.'

'Do you find Michael Larkin guilty or not guilty of murder?'

'Guilty.'

'Do you find William Gould guilty or not guilty of murder?'

'Guilty.'

'Do you find Thomas Maguire guilty or not guilty of murder?'

'Guilty.'

'Do you find Edward Shore guilty or not guilty of murder?'

'Guilty.'

A ripple of applause issued from the public gallery. Then they heard sobbing. From the back of the gallery, a door closed.

The only sound now was the hiss of the gas jets. There was no movement. Now the agonising uncertainty was ended. The malicious glee of those in the public gallery seemed stifled.

'What have you to say why the court may not pass sentence of death on you?'

Allen stepped to the front of the dock and rested his hands on the rail. There was no tremor in them now or in his voice as he spoke. His face was flushed below his high cheekbones and he swept the black hair back from his brow with an impatient flick of his head.

'No man regrets the death of Sergeant Brett more than I do and I say positively in the presence of the Almighty and ever-living God, that I am innocent, aye, as innocent as any man in this court. I don't say this for the sake of mercy: I want no mercy – I'll have no mercy. I'll die as many thousands have died, for the sake of their beloved land, and in defence of it. I will die proudly and triumphantly in defence of republican principles and the liberty of an oppressed and enslaved people.

'Why, we are asked, should sentence of death not be passed on us on the evidence of prostitutes off the streets of Manchester and convicted felons. Aye, and Irishmen sentenced to be hung when an English dog would have got off. I say positively and defiantly, justice has not been done me.

'As for myself, I feel the righteousness of my every act with regard to what I have done in defence of my country.

I fear not. I am fearless – fearless of the punishment that can be inflicted on me.'

He bowed to the court and then stepped back. His place was taken by Larkin, who was even paler than he had been at the start of the trial. He looked about him at the upturned faces. His expression was that of a man who, by sheer willpower, has mastered the fear rending his body.

'I too have a word or two to say concerning Sergeant Brett. No one could regret the man's death as much as I do. I call God as my witness that I neither used pistols, revolvers or any instrument on that day that would deprive the life of a child, let alone a man. Nor did I go there to take life away. Certainly, I do not deny that I did go to give aid and assistance to those two noble heroes – Kelly and Deasy. I did go to do as much as lay in my power to extricate them from their bondage; but I did not go to take life – nor did anyone else. It is a misfortune there was life taken, but if it was taken it was not done intentionally and the man who has taken life we [*sic*] have not got him.' Larkin paused, allowing his claim that the man who shot Brett was not in the dock to register with the judges.

'So far as my noble counsel went, they done their utmost in the protection of my life; likewise, my worthy solicitor, Mr Roberts, has done his best. So now I look to the mercy of God. May God forgive all who have sworn my life away. As I am a dying man, I forgive them from the bottom of my heart. God forgive them.'

As Larkin stepped back from the rail, O'Brien tilted

his blonde head backwards. It was a slight, almost imperceptible gesture, but everyone in the court seemed to notice it and they gave him their attention.

He stood silently for a few moments. It was a trick he had learned when speaking to his men.

'Every witness who has sworn anything against me has sworn falsely. I have not had a stone in my hand since I was a boy. I had no pistol in my possession on the day when it is alleged this outrage was committed.

'The right of man is freedom. The great God has endowed him with affections that he might use, not smother, and a world that may be enjoyed. Once a man is satisfied he is doing right, and attempts to do anything with that conviction, he must be willing to face all the consequences. Ireland, with its beautiful scenery, its delightful climate, its rich and productive land, is capable of supporting more than treble its population in ease and comfort. Yet no man, except a paid official of the British government, can say there is a shadow of glad life among its plundered and persecuted inhabitants. It is to be hoped her imbecile and tyrannical rulers will be forever driven from her soil amidst the execration of the world. How beautifully the aristocrats of England moralise on the despotism of the rulers of Italy. Who has not heard their condemnation of the tyranny that would compel honourable and good men to spend their useful lives in hopeless banishment?'

Blackburn spoke.

'I appeal to the prisoner, entirely for his own sake,

to cease his remarks. The only possible effects of your observations must be to tell against you with those who have to consider the sentence. I advise you to say nothing more of that sort. I do so entirely for your own sake.'

'Well, sir, I prefer saying it,' O'Brien said.

Blackburn withdrew his hands from his desk and sat back.

'These English hypocrites shriek in horror at the cruelty of foreign kings, but why don't they look at home and see those greater crimes committed by their government and with their sanction? Let them look at London and see the thousands that want bread there while those aristocrats are rioting in luxuries and crimes. Look to Ireland; see the hundreds of thousands of people in misery and want. See the virtuous, beautiful and industrious women who only a few years ago – aye, and still – are obliged to look at their children dying for want of food. Look at what is called the majesty of the law on one side and the long deep misery of a noble people on the other. Which are the young men of Ireland to respect – the law that murders and banishes their people or the means to resist relentless tyranny? The Irish people will answer this question soon.

'I am not astonished at my conviction. I am confident that my blood will rise a hundredfold against the tyrants who consider it proper to commit such an outrage. I was identified wrongly – the witnesses who have sworn to my throwing stones and firing a pistol have sworn to what is false. I thank my counsel for their able defence and also Mr Roberts for his attention to my case.'

Maguire spoke next. He stepped up to the bar with surprising assurance and his voice was calm and steady.

'I have been away from this place. I have been in the *Princess Royal* in China and Japan and I came home to see my friends on furlough. The witnesses who swore against me have perjured themselves. It is a false identity altogether with regard to me. I had not been out of my house until seven that night when I went to a music hall and did not leave until over half past ten.

'I won't tell no lies. It is a false identity, a mistaken identity, the Lord knows, this blessed and holy night. There was never one of my family connected with Fenianism as far as I know. I have always behaved myself to my queen and country and if I had not a good character I should not have been taken on for a second period.

'If there was ever an innocent man before you at the bar, I am an innocent man. I never was near the place and I would not know the way to Belle Vue. I would not know the direction if I was shown it.

'I have got no more to say but I give my best thanks to Mr Jones and Mr Roberts who have conducted the case; but it is a false identity with regard to me altogether.'

Then Condon stepped to the bar. A smile played across his lips – the smile of a man who does not expect the world to be any better than it is and who is amused by any man's hope that it might be.

'With regard to the unfortunate man who has lost his life, I sympathise with him and his family as deeply as anyone in this court. I deeply regret the unfortunate occurrence but I am as innocent of his blood as any man. I never had the slightest intention of taking life. I do not desire to be accused of a murder I have not committed. I leave this world without a stain on my conscience. I am totally guiltless. I leave this world without malice to anyone. I do not accuse the jury but I believe they were prejudiced. Every one of the witnesses has sworn falsely. I never threw a stone or fired a pistol. But as I have to go before my God, I forgive them. Had I committed anything against the crown of England I would have scorned myself had I attempted to deny it. Yet, innocent as I am, I was arrested and in consequence of the rewards which were offered I was identified. We have been found guilty and, as a matter of course, we accept death as gracefully as possible. We are not afraid to die – at least I am not.'

'Nor I.'

'Nor I.'

'Nor I.'

Maguire made no response.

'I have no stain upon me and I leave the world at peace with all.

'With regard to the other prisoners who are to be tried afterwards I hope our blood will satisfy the craving for it. I hope our blood will be enough and those other men will get a fair, free and a more impartial trial.

'I too, like my friend here,' he indicated O'Brien with a gesture, 'am an American citizen. I belong to Ohio and there are loving hearts there that will be sorry for this. I can assure them I die as a Christian and an Irishman and that I am not afraid or ashamed of the consequences of anything I have done before God or man. They would be ashamed of me if I was in the slightest degree a coward or concealed my opinions. You will soon send us before God and I am perfectly prepared to go. I have nothing to regret or retract. I can only say, God save Ireland.'

'God save Ireland,' the men in the dock echoed.

'I would be most happy and nothing would give me greater pleasure than to die on the field for my country in defence of her liberty. As it is I cannot die on the field but I can die on the scaffold, I hope, as a soldier, a man and a Christian.'

Condon stepped back from the bar.

The court sank into silence. A ragged volley of coughs pointed up the silence. The shuffling stopped and the usher moved towards the bench. The judges placed the black caps on their wigs. Mr Justice Mellor spoke.

'Yours is a crime which has struck at the very foundations of society. No person who has witnessed these proceedings can doubt the propriety of the verdict, which is the result of a full, patient and impartial investigation. I am perfectly convinced that all of you had resolved, at any risk, and by any amount of dangerous violence and outrage, to accomplish your object; and that, in fact, Charles Brett was murdered because it was essential to the completion of your common design that he should be.

'I recommend you to repair to the Cross of Christ with prayer and penitence.

'The sentence is that you, and each of you, be taken hence to the place whence you came, and then to a place of execution, and that you be hanged by the neck until you shall be dead and that your bodies be afterwards buried within the precincts of the prison wherein you were last confined after your respective convictions; and may God, in His infinite mercy, have mercy upon you.'

The time set for the execution was eight o'clock on the morning of Saturday 23 November.

The prisoners said nothing. As they left each leaned over the bar and shook the hands of his legal representatives. Jones still had about him the look of fixed determination that had characterised his actions.

'This is just the beginning,' he said, his face resolutely set in a smile, as if defying the men to challenge his optimism.

Roberts' warm smile framed a conspiratorial wink. 'This is only the first round.'

The court was silent. The only sound was the soft sobbing of a woman in the public gallery.

8

TWENTY-ONE DAYS

While the 'principal defendants' awaited execution, the trial of the others charged in connection with the death of Sergeant Brett continued. Kerslake and Mellor returned to London. Mr Justice Blackburn, having already dismissed all charges against John Bacon – the lame man accused of encouraging those who were attacking the van – for lack of evidence, also directed the release of John Francis Nugent, John Brannon, Timothy Featherstone, William Martin and Patrick Coffey, who were found not guilty of murder. Nugent was immediately arrested by Thomas Welby, head chief constable of the Irish constabulary, and charged with involvement in the Fenian rising in Drogheda in March 1867.

On the same day a further batch of defendants, Thomas Scalley, Henry Wilson, Michael Joseph Boylan, Michael McGuire and William Murphy, previously charged with murder, were cleared of this charge as no evidence was offered against them.

Bombs were found in Liverpool that day and reserve

forces were placed at the city's ten principal police stations and kept on duty around the clock.

On 13 November the commission found against John Carroll, Charles Moorhouse, Daniel Reddin, Thomas Scalley, William Murphy, John Brannon and Timothy Featherstone, who were all convicted of assaulting the police and doing grievous bodily harm. Featherstone and Murphy, when acquitted of murder, had immediately been charged with the lesser offence.

Mr Justice Blackburn was unhappy with the outcome and made his dissatisfaction clear: 'Although the Crown has chosen not to proffer the charge of murder ... I cannot doubt that every one of you is really guilty in part of the murder of Brett.' He then sentenced each to five years' penal servitude, the maximum penalty the law allowed.

William Murphy protested that the only evidence against him was the nationalist newspaper the police found in his possession when they arrested him. Years later, having served his sentence, Murphy told the Fenian John Denvir that it would have been his proudest boast to have said that he was present at the rescue but in fact he wasn't.

Daniel Reddin, who had been singled out by Edward Condon as a man of great courage, became gravely ill and partially paralysed because of his treatment in prison. Released on compassionate grounds, he deteriorated rapidly and died within a few months.

While the trial was going on police arrested Colonel

Ricard O'Sullivan Burke, the man who had acquired the guns for the Manchester Fenians. Godfrey Massey, a Fenian informer, helped to identify him.

Four months later, in March 1868, two other men were tried at Manchester Assizes in connection with the rescue. Daniel Darragh, who appeared under the alias of William Thompson, and Patrick Melody were sentenced to death for their role in procuring arms but their sentences were commuted to penal servitude for life. Darragh died in Portland Prison on 28 June 1870. His remains were returned to his family in Ballycastle, County Antrim, where they lie under a monument.

John Devoy claimed that Patrick Melody was never a Fenian, merely a bar-room patriot who had lived in London since leaving Ireland and had never set foot in Manchester. Nevertheless, one evening Patrick told his drinking cronies – in the strictest confidence – of his role in the rescue. The next day police arrested him and whisked him off to Manchester where an array of witnesses swore to his participation in the rescue. The court convicted him and he served ten years' penal servitude.

NEW BAILEY PRISON, SALFORD,
SATURDAY 2 NOVEMBER 1867

The masons and joiners were building the scaffold. It would hang sixty feet above the front of the New Bailey Prison with a platform for troops running the full length of the wall on both sides and reached by stairs from the prison yard. Maddeningly Allen, himself a joiner, caught a whiff of white pine on the air and moved to the window, filling his lungs, half expecting to find blonde curls of timber shavings on the sill.

Before they'd arrived back at prison after the verdict, the condemned men had worked it out: it was twenty-one days to the execution. For each of them there was now a new calendar, which consisted not of months and weeks but was instead marked out by the appallingly short span of days which separated them from abrupt and certain death. The future was twenty-one days.

From the instant that the sentence of death first hung over them they no longer owned their own thoughts. Serenity fled. Every waking minute stank of death. First thing in the morning, in those seconds immediately after waking, it would sometimes exist only as a throbbing limb, a floating dread. Momentarily it seemed merely a memory of a memory. Then it hit like a fist in the face and immediately pervaded everything. Fr Gadd became the lifeboat to which they clung in the enraged ocean that daily threatened to overwhelm them. He was a curate at St John's Cathedral, Salford, and Catholic chaplain to the New Bailey. When the men were convicted, he rushed back from his holidays at Limerick Junction and began making them ready for death. During the final few days, Fr Quick, from St Wilfred's parish, Hulme, and Fr Edward Cantwell, from St Patrick's, Rochdale Road, helped him prepare the men.

Fr Gadd's monumental serenity infused their devotions. They celebrated Mass every morning and every second day received Holy Communion. They examined their consciences, confessed their sins, prayed, meditated on Christ's passion, death and resurrection, recited the Rosary, contemplated passages from scripture and examined their past lives. And though death remained ever present, the balm of faith masked it.

Occasionally, an unaccountable optimism flared. 'They'll not hang us,' said Allen, turning his head with contempt at the very thought of it. 'They wouldn't dare.' Allen's confidence was more than the bravado of despair. An objective assessment of the situation provided grounds for optimism and there were many prominent public figures determined to exhaust every means of ensuring a reprieve.

James Finlen was typical of many of those who took up the cause of the condemned men. Like his former colleague on the *People's Paper*, Ernest Jones, he too was a prominent Chartist and a powerful advocate for the Reform League, which was campaigning for the extension of the franchise. The fact that he was an Irishman and a republican no doubt reinforced his fervour and moved him to hold what he called an 'indignation meeting' in the anteroom of the Home Office when Home Secretary Gathorne-Hardy denied his request for a meeting.

Many others besieged Gathorne-Hardy with requests for a hearing and pleas for clemency. Among these were not only the Catholic hierarchy and many individual parish priests, but other religious organisations, representing Quakers and Dissenters, and many Church of England parish priests acting on their own initiative. The Reform League and the General Council of the International Working Men's Association added their weight to the campaign, as was to be expected, though it is doubtful that these last two had any influence on Lord Derby's Tory government, associated as they were with the cause of universal suffrage and the ideas of Marx and Engels respectively.

It is indicative of the extent of opposition to the executions that five MPs, many justices of the peace, several lawyers and the Cork Chamber of Commerce, together with groups of prominent Manchester businessmen, also asked the government to commute the sentences. As late as Thursday 21 November, two days before the scheduled executions, the Manchester Corn Exchange hosted a public meeting which despatched a deputation to the home secretary on behalf of the condemned men.

News of these petitions and deputations, assiduously passed on to the condemned men by Fr Gadd and the others who were ministering to them, certainly buoyed their spirits. The priest repeatedly reminded them that though they must prepare for the worst they had good reason to hope for a reprieve.

One thing that certainly encouraged their hopes was the attitude of the press. It was widely assumed in Ireland that none of the five would hang on such a 'broken-down verdict'. Typical of the encouraging opinions expressed at the end of the trial was that of the local paper, the *Manchester Examiner*. 'We do not for a moment imagine the capital penalty will be carried out ... but we none the less wish the verdict had commended itself on more satisfactory grounds to the confidence of the public.'

Others went further. *Reynold's News* described the verdict as a 'disgrace to Britain' which refusal to commute the sentences of the condemned would merely compound.

More than anything else the conviction of Thomas Maguire, who was patently innocent, undermined the credibility of the case against the others. Many outside Fenian and even Irish circles were outraged at Maguire's situation. Sections of the British press started to question the verdict. *The Manchester Guardian*, for instance, speaking of Maguire said, 'His conviction goes to prove that the panic-stricken Manchester jury was determined to convict and hang every man put in the dock alongside Allen.'

Thousands – including the lord mayor of Manchester, local councillors and MPs – signed the petition requesting Maguire's release. His neighbours, many of them English, supported by local businessmen, drew up a plea for clemency and thirty of the forty journalists who covered the trial took the unprecedented step of petitioning the Home Secretary, stating that Maguire was the innocent victim of mistaken identity. The implication of this was not lost on the government: had not the judges said that they 'fully concur in the verdict of the jury'? What's more, if their judgement with regard to Maguire was so grotesque, what reason was there to believe it was not similarly flawed with regard to the other men who had been convicted on the evidence of the same witnesses who were sending Maguire to the gallows?

As the campaign gathered momentum, newspaper revelations about the character of some of the witnesses further undermined their credibility in the eyes of the public. Many were exposed in the press as thieves, pickpockets, habitual drunkards or criminals seeking to ingratiate themselves with the police.

There was also some legal basis for challenging the validity of the conviction. There was at that time no such thing as a court of appeal and no means of appealing even a sentence of death. Yet the defence continued to make the argument they had put to Blackburn and Mellor during the trial: because of deficiencies in the warrants, the authorities had exceeded their powers in holding Kelly and Deasy and therefore those who freed them should not have been charged with murder but with manslaughter. The procedure for assessing such a claim depended entirely on the view of the trial judges: if they believed the claim worthy of consideration they could refer it to the Court of Crown Cases Reserved for judgement.

Not surprisingly, as Blackburn had explicitly denounced the implication of the defence interpretation of the precedents as 'monstrous', he and Mr Justice Mellor ruled against referral. With this decision the supporters of the condemned men turned their attention to other avenues. What they sought, after all, was not by any means exceptional. At that time about half of those sentenced to death had their sentence commuted. What's more, the general tenor of opinion among the political elite was moving against the routine execution of convicted murderers. A recent royal commission had recommended that only certain categories of murderers should suffer the ultimate penalty. This case was exactly the type they had in mind for lesser penalties as the men stood convicted of constructive murder – an offence for which no one had previously hanged.

However, the most compelling reason for seeking a commutation of sentence had nothing to do with these issues, which might apply to any murder trial. It was the political nature of their crime. As O'Brien pointed out from the dock, Britain's liberal press lionised the followers of Mazzini and other continental nationalists who took up arms in the cause of national independence. Besides, the last Irishman executed for such a crime was Robert Emmet in 1803, and even reactionary politicians believed that it was generally counter-productive to make martyrs of one's political enemies.

What's more, hanging Michael O'Brien and Edward Condon might put further strain on already fraught Anglo-American relations. Both were American citizens and veterans of the Civil War and the men's supporters had asked the American government to intervene on their behalf.

However, not all influences were pushing in favour of the men. Events in the Commons in the week after the commission delivered its verdict indicated that the government did not intend to give those campaigning for a reprieve an easy victory.

That Thursday, but for a scattering of members, most reading, others with batons of order papers in their hands, the House was empty. When Sir Patrick O'Brien, the last of the three MPs to urge a reprieve, had resumed his seat, Gathorne-Hardy stood. In two strides he was at the despatch box. The expression on his face was that of a man with a troublesome tooth.

He dispensed the ritual pleasantries – the views of the honourable members carefully considered, their contribution most welcome, their opinions valued. He spoke like a defeated captain praising his opponent's victory. Then his tone changed. 'However, I regret that after long and careful consideration, I see no reason to recommend any delay to the executions.'

The execution was to go ahead, as scheduled, on Saturday 23 November.

NEW BAILEY PRISON, WEDNESDAY 13 NOVEMBER
Allen's fiancée, Mary Ann Hickey, visited him. Throughout the meeting, for long periods, she wept uncontrollably. When he succeeded in consoling her, Allen repeated what he had already told his mother: that he felt no guilt for the death of Sergeant Brett and that the man who shot

him had escaped and was not among those charged with involvement in the rescue.

Maguire, more than any of the others, was racked by the excruciating uncertainty. Fr Gadd tried to sustain him by recounting news of every petition, demonstration and appeal on his behalf. One effect of this, however, was to increase his monomania: he was preoccupied every waking minute with the injustice of his conviction, the refusal of the court to believe those who provided his alibi and the increasing possibility that, though no one other than those who convicted and sentenced him believed he was guilty, he would nevertheless die on the gallows.

NEW BAILEY PRISON, FRIDAY 15 NOVEMBER

Larkin's mother, who was recently widowed, his wife and their four young children – the youngest a babe in arms – visited him. More than anything else he was tormented by the realisation that his death would condemn them to a life of destitution. He knew that with him gone, the workhouse awaited them.

NEW BAILEY PRISON, MONDAY 18 NOVEMBER

Allen wrote to his sister, brothers and brother-in-law:

> It is hard to be suffering for a charge one is not guilty of. I am reconciled to the will of God, whatever my fate might be. I received holy communion this morning and am in very good spirits. Tell my brothers to mind their duty to God and

always pray for me and all that are in with me. Remember my words, dear friends – there is no use in grieving at all. It does not make the thing any better, and injures your own health, although I am quite sure there will be many thousands that never saw me or any of the other prisoners in their lives, that will regret our deaths; and many a tear will flow from parties with whom I never was in my life. I am about to leave the world and I do not think that I have many enemies in it except those that swore my life away for blood money. I forgive them from the bottom of my heart and may God forgive them.

Allen was prone to violent swings of emotion – one minute euphoric, adamant he would not die, certain the government would see the folly of executing them, would bend to the clamour for a reprieve or simply have a change of heart; an hour later a suffocating despair left him unable to talk and he was full of resentful envy of those prisoners he heard in other parts of the prison who had only to let time pass, knowing they had a future beyond this place. At such times he damned all the talk of reprieve as nothing more than added agony, mocking torture that served only to ratchet up his suffering and lift him to a greater height from which he would plunge. Then he would examine the marks on the bed, table and stool, the patina of wear made by the hands of former prisoners and wonder about those men and where they were.

Where would they bury him? How could he, not yet a

man, a mere nineteen years of age, die? His life had hardly begun. He had so many things to do – he was to marry and hoped to see Ireland free.

Between him and all that, however, stood William Calcraft, the official executioner, one of the most infamous men in England, the focus of a grim, insatiable fascination. When the men awaiting Calcraft in the New Bailey thought of him, they thought of only one of the myriad details of his life with which the newspapers regaled their readers – not his love of children or his passion for flowers or even his famous harness for fastening his victims: they thought only of his reputation for botching executions. They all knew the stories of his victims slowly throttled, their necks crushed by imperceptible degrees by the weight of their own writhing bodies.

Heedless of the campaign for reprieve, preparations for the execution went on apace. Salford magistrates swore in 1,000 special constables to guard the approaches to the place of execution. The Manchester papers reported that the specials were plentifully fed with hot pork pies and beer.

Meanwhile, the life of the prison went on. The sound of hammers and saws filled the air as the building of the scaffold, the sixty-foot staircase and the parapet went on throughout the daylight hours. At night the cries of troubled dreamers broke the silence of the prison. During those dark hours, most of the warders were home, drinking sweet tea in front of warm hearths, children on their knees.

From beyond the walls of the prison the condemned men could hear the clatter of hooves and the cries of cabmen carrying people home or to business in the city's sumptuous hotels, the Midland or the Grand. For those people the executions were merely another item in the newspaper, like the weather forecast or a sale of cattle in Cheshire.

NEW BAILEY PRISON, WEDNESDAY 20 NOVEMBER

Larkin's uncle and three cousins visited him in his cell. The five sat in a circle, their heads bent towards each other, and spoke earnestly of how they would help the condemned man's wife and children. They spoke for several hours and when they left the little tailor seemed encouraged by what they had told him.

The same day Allen's mother visited him. She was re-strained and calm. O'Brien and Condon had no visitors on this or any other day except Fr Gadd, who spent most of the day with them. As one newspaper said, Fr Gadd was 'unremitting in his attention to the men since their condemnation'.

A proclamation by the mayor of Salford appeared on the prison wall that night, announcing that the execution was to take place three days hence at eight o'clock, on the morning of Saturday 23 November. It asked all 'well-disposed inhabitants of the borough' to stay away.

CLERKENWELL, LONDON,
WEDNESDAY 20 NOVEMBER

A river of fire, like a rush of molten lead, burned a fissure through the winter night. On and on it came, twisting, contorting through the narrow Clerkenwell streets.

No one spoke. The only sound was the shuffle of boots and the hiss of the torches in the narrow streets. The men held the flames above their heads. Beneath the canopy of fire, their cavernous eyes looked at the bewildered spectators scattered along the kerbside. The flames cast a sudden dawn into darkened bedrooms and threw the twisted parallelograms of window frames onto a thousand ceilings.

At last, the men turned off the main road into the park, where the darkness thickened under the great oaks. Ahead of them, on a platform six feet above the ground, three figures stood dark against the night sky. Then the marching men formed up, phalanx upon phalanx, a hundred bodies deep and twice as wide.

Now the light lapped the men on the podium. Two stood at the front, their lean frock-coated bodies bent towards the light, their hair restive in the damp breeze.

Mr Clegg spoke first. He told the gathered crowd of the petition sponsored not only by the working men of every great British city but also by the leading citizens of Manchester. Extending his left arm to the man beside him, he commended Mr Finlen to them. Finlen was working tirelessly on behalf of the Manchester prisoners and had agreed to lead a deputation to the Home Secretary, Gathorne-Hardy, on their behalf.

Clegg next said he was honoured to introduce Charles Bradlaugh MP. Bradlaugh was a champion of the working man, but they all knew he was renowned for something else – he had defied God. Once he had stood in a main road challenging God to prove His existence by striking him dead. Now this man, who feared nothing, prepared to address them.

As Bradlaugh's fierce eyes glowered down on them from a face swathed in a black beard, some of the men flinched, no doubt fearful that he might again test God and bring down a curse on their cause.

NEW BAILEY PRISON, THURSDAY 21 NOVEMBER, 10.00 A.M.

Two days before he was to die Maguire heard the sound of the key in his cell door. He lurched to his feet.

'Any news, Father?' But it wasn't Fr Gadd.

'Stand back against the wall,' said the turnkey.

The governor winced as he stepped into the cell. Lifting his handkerchief to his nose, he took half a pace back into the corridor.

'I have news, Maguire.' The governor coughed and dabbed his nose with the handkerchief. 'It has pleased Her Majesty's government to grant you a free pardon. You are to be released immediately. The government has been persuaded by those who petitioned on your behalf that your conviction is unsafe.'

Maguire swayed and folded to his knees. 'Thanks be to God,' he whimpered, crossing himself. He looked up into the governor's eyes. 'Thank you, sir. God bless you, sir.' He started to shuffle towards the governor, his hands raised in incredulous gratitude, his face wet with tears.

'Back against the wall,' said the turnkey, drawing his truncheon.

Ten minutes later, Maguire stepped out through the small door cut in the prison's large outer gate. It snapped shut behind him as he stood on New Bailey Street watching men and women moving purposefully to their work, paying him no heed. Though the light was still grainy and the sky pregnant with rain, the day was mild and he opened his coat. After so long he was aware of the novelty of walking and conscious of the muscles in his legs working as he put one foot in front of the other and turned towards his sister's house in Greengate.

His heart beat fast, sweat glazed his brow and as he approached Chapel Street he noticed two street urchins, who had been rolling a brown beer bottle to each other across the paving flags, looking at him. He felt a twinge of recognition – were they the children of one of his sister's neighbours? They pointed at him.

'Hey, mister,' the taller of the two called, 'they was going to hang you.'

'Have you got away?' the smaller one asked.

'They've let me off, thank God,' said Maguire. 'They found out I was telling the truth and let me off.'

'The sailor's got off,' the taller cried, 'the sailor's got off.' The younger lad took up the cry and started chanting rhythmically, 'the sailor's got off, the sailor's got off'. They bounced up and down on the balls of their grubby bare feet, chanting, 'the sailor's got off, the sailor's got off'.

BIRMINGHAM, THURSDAY 21 NOVEMBER

Not everyone shared the children's delight. Among many sections of British society there was vehement opposition to Maguire's reprieve. Nowhere was this more evident than in Birmingham.

The first stone took off the outstretched arm of Jesus. The second hit the sill of the nave window with a puff of sandstone. Then a volley of rocks exploded against the timber doors of St Chad's Cathedral.

'No pope in Birmingham!' cried a scrawny man with a billycock hat and mutton-chop whiskers. He loped from the front of the crowd and swung his arm like a fast bowler, flighting his stone into the dead centre of the triptych above the high altar. It punched a hole in Gabriel's wing.

All around him men and boys broke from the crowd and hurled stones at will. The sound of glass falling inside the cathedral punctuated the thuds against the sandstone walls. Soon the shower became a torrent. The stones pecked away at the stained glass and then thunked against the lead lattice. They skipped off the sides of the building and spat up the gravel on the path around the cathedral.

'Come out, you bastards.'

'Get back to your pig sties!'

'England for the English!'

Now the stone-throwers stood panting round the edges of the crowd, their arms resting on their knees, their shoulders pumping.

'Bugger me stiff,' cried a young man with a tuft of yellow hair on top of his long head. 'It's the peelers.'

A hundred stones fell to the ground as pushing and jostling the crowd turned, and in a great tangle of buffeting shoulders fled down the road.

NEW BAILEY PRISON, THURSDAY 21 NOVEMBER

Maguire's release caused a change of mood among the men: all four now accepted that they would die on Saturday morning.

Then, at 1.15 p.m., Fr Gadd brought the news to Condon in his cell: because of intervention by the American ambassador, the government had commuted his sentence to penal servitude for life. Condon knew exactly what this meant.

The government had introduced penal servitude to replace transportation. Under this regime convicts spent the first part of their sentence in solitary confinement. For the remainder they laboured on public works. For ordinary prisoners there was hope: provided their behaviour was exemplary, they won release on 'ticket of leave' – a form of parole that depended on their continued good conduct. This, of course, was something Condon could not hope for.

It was during this period that Dartmoor – originally built for French prisoners during the Napoleonic Wars – was opened as a government prison.

This regime of hard physical labour in a spartan institution became infamous because of the experiences of another Fenian, Jeremiah O'Donovan Rossa, whose accounts of his time in Millbank Prison, smuggled out by sympathisers, sparked international outrage. O'Donovan Rossa told of the treatment inflicted on him and other Fenians: packed with others into a room the size of a broom cupboard with barely enough room to breathe; weeks in solitary; naked in his cell, hands cuffed behind his back, lapping his bread and water from a plate on the floor like a dog.

Fr Gadd, however, made no mention of any of this, though it was common knowledge among Fenians. Instead he repeatedly told the men that this was far more significant than Maguire's reprieve. Maguire was totally innocent: he had played no part in the rescue. Condon, however, had planned the entire thing and at his trial had proudly affirmed his role. Having reprieved him, Fr Gadd explained, Gathorne-Hardy was now under increasing pressure to save the others.

The news, however, unsettled Allen, Larkin and O'Brien. Fighting to suppress hope, they found it springing up again, a tortuous tease, mocking their resolve, unravelling their resignation. It was the most exquisite torture yet. And in fact, later that very day, Fr Gadd brought a letter to

Michael O'Brien from the American ambassador. It began by reminding O'Brien that in 1866 he had intervened on his behalf when he stood accused of building up a Fenian arms cache. At that time the ambassador warned him that he should stay out of trouble and made it clear that the American government would not again support him should he break British laws. 'Unfortunately,' the ambassador's letter concluded, 'you chose not to heed that prudent advice.'

'This is not the end, Michael,' Fr Gadd assured him. Many others were working tirelessly on his behalf, the priest reminded him. To O'Brien, however, it felt like the end. The country for which he had risked his life had abandoned him. He'd allowed hope to escape its confines and now it mocked him, jeered at his folly and tortured him more than at any time since the sentence was passed.

NEW BAILEY PRISON, FRIDAY 22 NOVEMBER, 10.00 A.M.

Allen's sister and cousin and Larkin's two sisters-in-law arrived at the prison. The governor refused them entry.

Later, Allen's fiancée, Mary Ann Hickey, arrived. She was weeping uncontrollably. The governor turned her away too.

Inside already were Larkin's mother, wife and children. A journalist who saw them waiting inside the gates said 'a more heart-tearing scene I never witnessed'.

Later the prison authorities sent a message to Allen's mother, informing her that the governor had granted her leave to visit her son.

When Allen's and Larkin's visitors left, the men spent all their time with their priests.

NEW BAILEY, FRIDAY 22 NOVEMBER, 12.30 P.M.
William Calcraft and his assistant, Armstrong, arrived unobserved at the New Bailey. Calcraft was sixty-seven years old and had held his position as public executioner since 1829. He was the focus of intense public interest, one of the celebrities of the day, an object of fascination and hatred. This was in large measure because of his famed incompetence at his trade. The 'short drop' technique he employed often failed to break the victim's neck and kill instantly; instead the victim died of slow strangulation.

LONDON, FRIDAY 22 NOVEMBER
A deputation from the Manchester Corn Exchange arrived in Whitehall to present a petition to the home secretary. Gathorne-Hardy refused to see them.

On the same day the home secretary received letters of protest from the Bishops of Cashel, Killaloe and Derry; John Bright, famous radical and co-founder of the Anti-Corn Law League; J. S. Mill, philosopher and MP; and the poet Algernon Swinburne.

The same day Mr Finlen's deputation from Clerkenwell arrived at the gates of Windsor Castle, where Queen Victoria was in residence. A mob lay in wait and attacked them. Later in the day they returned. The queen refused to see them.

New Bailey, Friday 22 November

The men awaiting execution were overwhelmed by inertia, as if in a drug-induced stupor. They felt as if all their exertions, the extremes of emotion and the tension had drained their energy and left them exhausted. Others might fight on their behalf but they were no longer capable of any effort. Their struggle was over.

That evening Allen wrote to his Uncle and Aunt Hogan: 'I am dying for Ireland, dying for the Ireland of saints, dying for liberty. Every generation of our countrymen is suffering and where is the Irish heart that could stand by unmoved?'

He forgave those who swore his life away and asked God to forgive them. 'I am dying, thank God, an Irishman and a Christian.'

Salford Town Hall, Friday 22 November, 2.30 p.m.

That afternoon the Mayor of Salford met the magistrates and the head constable, Captain Sylvester, to finalise the arrangements for the defence of the prison in the event of a Fenian rescue attempt. A reserve occupied the nearby Salford Station. For the protection of the area immediately around the prison they deployed a detachment of the 57th Regiment, the 72nd Highlanders, the 8th Hussars and a company of the Royal Artillery with two batteries of guns. Some of these were to occupy both the Lancashire and Yorkshire and the London and North West Railway bridges which commanded the approaches to the prison. Stationed in the prison itself were a reserve of the line, and two detachments, one of artillery and another of cavalry. Major-General Sir John Garvock, commander-in-chief of the northern district, finally approved the arrangements. Everything was in place to repel any last-ditch Fenian rescue bid.

NEW BAILEY PRISON, FRIDAY 22 NOVEMBER, 4.00 P.M.

'Thanks be to God,' said Larkin, his eyes now wild and bright like a consumptive's. 'Our prayers are answered.' He clasped his hands and dropped to his knees. Fr Gadd knelt beside him. He opened the letter and reread it. The paper was heavy and thick. Never before had he seen paper like it. His eye fell on the signature, the great swirling 'Q' elaborate and confident.

'Who is this Caroline Queensberry? Why should she do this?'

'The Marchioness of Queensberry is a decent, compassionate woman,' said Fr Gadd. 'The woman is a true Catholic, Mikey, and a fine example to us all. She read about you in the papers – the English papers – and despite their lies and bigotry, she saw the truth. God inspired her to take pity on your wife and children.'

'God bless her, Father. May God smile on her and hers.' His eyes fixed on the line 'so long as I live they shall be cared for to the utmost of my power'.

'Is it true, Father?'

'It is, Mikey. Rest assured, you need have no concern for your family. The woman sent McDonnell, her personal envoy. They are in the best of hands. And not only that, but look, she has Mass said for you every day.'

'And she provided one hundred pounds in cash for my family?'

'I saw it with my own eyes. Isn't God wondrous how he achieves His purposes, Mikey?'

'I can do it now, Father. I'm certain I can. Without a doubt.'

'What's that, Mikey?'

'Now I can go to my death like a man. I have no worries. My conscience is clear and my family will not want.' Holding the letter at arm's length, he read from it. 'Today thou shalt be with me in Paradise.' He spoke like a man entranced.

'Christ will call you, Mikey.' The priest's voice was a whisper, barely audible. Their heads were close together. Larkin lifted his face and looked directly into the priest's tired eyes. For the first time Larkin noticed their colour: translucent blue, the colour of the sky on a clear December day. 'He'll be there, Mikey, His arms wide open, waiting for you.' Larkin could smell the sweet odour of the altar wine on the priest's breath. He closed his eyes and inhaled slowly.

The memory of the dry incense came back to him. The brilliant white of the altar server's chasuble over the black soutane, as he swung the silver censor, emitting a swan's feather of smoke; the golden candlesticks; the dancing flames, swaying in the draft; the silver tapestry of the priest's vestments and the voices, filling the nave, like the voice of Gabriel, high and low and clear, flooded back to him.

4.30 P.M.

Calcraft too had a letter. He stood in the light from the barred window and opened it with the care of a man who seldom receives mail. He raised it to his face, myopically, the rim of his beard touching the bottom of the page.

Armstrong studied his face. Large, flat and pale with pained, colourless eyes and framed by a grey beard, it was the bland face of an unworldly man, with the untested probity of a benevolent schoolmaster. He squinted and his brow creased. The tremor in his hand was now a shake and the rustle of the paper was audible. He thrust it from his face, holding it at arm's length.

'They say they'll kill me, they do.' The voice was high-pitched and strained. 'Those damn Fenians are going to kill me. Listen,' Calcraft said, reading from the page, '"Sir – If you hang any of the gentlemen condemned to death at the New Bailey Prison you will not survive afterwards".'

Calcraft immediately sent the note to the visiting justices of the gaols, adding, 'I have received the enclosed letter. It seems a serious job. I hope you will look after it that I shall get home safe again.'

4.45 P.M.

Outside, in preparation for the execution, the Salford authorities placed a barricade in the middle of New Bailey Street and stationed artillery in Stanley Street, near the entrance to the prison. They also blocked Bridge Street, Lower King Street, Albert Street, Gartside Street and Water Street at the bridge into New Bailey Street: the police now controlled every street leading to the prison. Captain Palin and Captain Sylvester, head constable of the Salford police, worked far into the night. They were finalising the deployment of the 500 officers and 2,000 special constables at their disposal.

They ordered ten officers to erect a barrier in front of the prison wall directly under where the carpenters had that afternoon finished erecting the drop.

5.30 P.M.

Allen took the steel-nibbed pen, its shaft blotched with black ink. Fr Gadd uncorked the ink and placed it on the small deal table under the gaslight. The blue flame hissed.

'In a few hours time I will be going before my God,' Allen wrote, his hand moving slowly over the page, his eyes wide with concentration:

I state in the presence of that great God that I am not the man who shot Sergeant Brett. If that man's wife is alive, never let her think that I am the person who deprived her of her husband. With the help of the Great God I am only dying to a world of sorrow to rise to a world of joy. Before the judgement seat of God there will be no false witnesses tolerated; everyone must render an account for himself.

I forgive all the enemies I ever had in this world. May God forgive them. Forgive them, sweet Jesus, forgive them. I also ask pardon of all whom I have injured in any way.

May the Lord have mercy on our souls and deliver Ireland from her sufferings. God save Ireland!

He signed it William Philip Allen.

In the next cell Larkin sat down at his table. His fingers were long and fine, the fingers of a tailor. He carefully scraped the excess ink from the underside of the nib. Then in his clear, neat hand, he began to write:

Men of the world – I as a dying man, going before my God, solemnly declare I have never fired a shot in all my life, much less the day the attack was made on the van … I am dying a patriot for my God and my country, and Larkin will be remembered in time to come by the sons and daughters of Erin.

Farewell dear Ireland, for I must leave you and die a martyr for your sake. Farewell dear mother, wife and children for I must leave you all for poor Ireland's sake. Farewell, uncles, aunts and cousins, likewise sons and daughters of Erin. I hope in heaven we will meet another day. God be with you. Father in heaven, forgive those that have sworn my life away. I forgive them and the world. God bless Ireland!

He read what he had written. He was pleased with it. It said all the things he would not have been able to speak. He wrote his name at the bottom: Michael Larkin.

Michael O'Brien too was writing. He bent his handsome head over the page. To those who would come after him and strive to redress all of Ireland's wrongs, he had already spoken. His words at the trial were for them. Now he wrote for himself:

> I did not use a revolver or any other firearm, or throw stones, on the day that Colonel Kelly and Captain Deasy were so gallantly rescued. I was not present when the van was attacked.
>
> I trust that those who swore to seeing me with a revolver were nothing more than mistaken. I forgive them from my heart; likewise I forgive all who have ever done me or intended to do me any injury.

O'Brien stretched forward and placed the pen carefully at the top of the table so it would not roll away.

6.30 P.M.

At the usual time, Mr Holt, the turnkey, locked each in his own cell, as he had done every evening at this time. Tonight was no different. But Holt's attitude had changed from the night they returned from the assize court under sentence of death: little courtesies, a certain compassion in the way he spoke, even apologising when he had to enforce a rule which seemed pointlessly cruel. From that first evening the condemned men were aware that there was a chasm separating them from other men.

Throughout the city the lights continued to burn in every factory and warehouse long after the machinery fell silent. The foremen and overseers were directing the hands as they barricaded windows and doors.

10.00 P.M.

The thoroughfares around the prison were filling up. At both ends of New Bailey Street special constables formed a line in front of the barricades. As the crowd thickened, hucksters did a brisk trade in hot potatoes, cans of beer, lumps of cheese, squares of bacon and boiled onions.

In the Albert Hotel, across the road from the prison, the last of the press men were arriving. They knew there would be few more days like this: liberal opinion was moving against the view that capital punishment was the only appropriate sentence for those convicted of homicide and was even more hostile to public executions.

From a journalistic perspective, this was a great pity. Nothing sold papers like a good execution. True, salacious court proceedings and brutal murders were good for business, but even they did not have the drama of an execution. Nothing could compete with the ultimate ordeal and the public's insatiable demand for information on the manner in which the condemned faced death. What else could gratify the public lust for righteous vengeance than the opportunity to see the guilty get their just deserts? And then there was that sense of superiority when they stepped out onto the scaffold: even the most verminous, destitute wretch would not swap places. What could ever take its place?

11.30 P.M.
'All's well,' came the cry from beyond the prison walls on the banks of the Irwell.

'All's well,' came its echo from inside the prison. Again, 'All's well,' this time more faintly, from the depths of the fortress.

One by one, the men fell asleep. They slept the sleep of exhaustion, a deep and dreamless sleep.

Stanley Street, in front of the prison, was barricaded at both ends and around midnight crowds began to form, pushing up against the barriers. They meandered out from the gin palaces and beer shops. The scaffold was draped in black. The police allowed the crowd to pass by but they were not allowed to stand still. The pubs in the area immediately around the prison filled up. Many people – dedicated execution goers – had come a long way and were anxious to get a good view.

NEW BAILEY PRISON, SATURDAY 23 NOVEMBER, 2.15 A.M.

All along the path between the Irwell and the prison flames from the great braziers contorted in the night air.

Below them the oily surface of the river seemed to blaze. The watchmen stood close around the fires, clapping their shoulders with gloved hands.

Occasionally a watchman walked down to the edge of the orbit of light and peered into the great black maw of the bridge that spanned the river on Bridge Street. The darkness gave up nothing other than the stink of putrefaction. No Fenians appeared. He hitched the rifle over his shoulder and turned, glad to be making his way back to the fire.

The soldier turned and looked down towards the bridge. Was something moving? Or was it the echo of the brazier spitting? He stood stock still. Listening.

STANLEY STREET, SALFORD, SATURDAY 23 NOVEMBER, 4 A.M.

The clock struck four. The spectators at the barriers across the end of Stanley Street looked up. Silhouetted against the night sky was the cross beam of the gibbet and the three nooses, each rope a different length. Beneath hung a great black awning, designed to conceal the prisoners when they fell through the drop. In the distance, from the far side of the prison, they heard the refrain: 'All's well.' It echoed through the building and then disappeared.

'Who do ye think you're pushing, ye cheeky little bleeder?' said the bleary-eyed man, turning in a wide circle like a dray horse. His momentum kept him turning and he held out his arms to steady himself.

'Where do you think you're goin', Sunshine?' The special constable placed his bulk self-importantly in the path of the boy who had insinuated his way between the packed bodies at the barrier.

'Special telegram, sir.' He lifted his right hand. Peeping out from the cylinder of his sleeve was the end of an envelope. 'For the governor, sir.' Only the boy's chin was visible between his peaked cap and his turned-up collar.

'Bugger me stiff,' said the bleary man, addressing the crowd, 'they've got off after all. Them bastards ain't going to swing.'

'They can't do that,' said a gaunt woman, her hands folded below her chin, 'We come all the way from Liverpool. They got no right to cancel it like that.'

A roar went up and the crowd surged forward. Hands clawed at the delivery boy, plucking at his coat. 'What does it say? What does it say?' they cried, lurching towards him. The special constables moved in, steering the boy under the barrier.

'Give it to the porter,' said the bulky constable, pointing. The boy ran for the lodge, an orb of warm light in the dank night, arms and legs stiff in his heavy coat. The porter opened the glass door. As the boy approached he lifted the letter towards him.

'What's the hurry, son?' asked the porter, examining the letter. The boy's breath came in plumes that swept over both of them.

'For the governor, sir.'

The porter held the envelope to his face as he scrutinised the big blue letters of the address that seemed to be written in crayon.

'It's come from London, sir,' said the boy.

Somewhere from the middle of the crowd, the plaintive squeak of a penny whistle rose. Then it started to pick out the staccato notes of 'Rule Britannia'. Immediately, the crowd joined in, bellowing the words to the night sky, bludgeoning out the rhythm with the pounding of boots on the stones and the beating of fists in the air. The end of the last chorus was greeted with a great drunken cheer and then, before the whooping had died, they took up the strains of 'The Men of Merrie England'. With hardly a break for breath they launched into 'John Brown's Bones' and then took up 'God Save the Queen'.

The singing ended with ragged cheers, clapping and backslapping. As the noise was ebbing away, those on the edge of the crowd called out.

'Listen!'

'Be quiet!'

'Shut up!'

The crowd fell quiet, only a few voices audible and then hushed to silence.

'What is it?'

'It's coming from over there – Blackfriars Street.'

Some arched their heads, scowling in concentration. Others peered towards Blackfriars Street, as if by looking they could hear the sound.

Suddenly some started. Some shuddered. Women tightened their shawls about them and shifted their feet. The men shrugged, as if someone had walked over their graves.

Now everyone could hear it. A woman wailing – and they'd never heard anything like it. It was a disembodied sound without any restraint, a naked cry of grief undiluted by any inhibition, the cry of pure desolation.

***

The singing went on all night. As the crowd grew, those coming from a night's drinking brought the atmosphere of the alehouse with them. They struck up one comic song after another.

The mist muffled the noise and as the darkness began to dissolve, it thickened, swaying in the air, mirrored in the frosty breath of the crowd. It clung to the black stone of the prison walls and snaked its way up to the top and around the parapet. The fresh timber was still pristine, the odour of wood shavings still hung in the air and the iron nail heads were not yet rusted. Along the Irwell the light from the braziers began to fade. The watchmen paced up and down, squinting into the arch of the bridge.

High above the river, the mist clouded the window of Allen's cell. The clock struck the quarter hour – 4.45. Allen was asleep under the coarse blanket, legs drawn up to his chest.

In the adjacent cells, O'Brien and Larkin were also

sleeping soundly. No dreams troubled their slumbers, nor did they cry out. Their breathing was slow and even, their bodies warm and slack. Deep in their sleep, they heard nothing.

9

VALIANT SOULS

New Bailey Prison, Saturday 23 November 1867, 4.45 a.m.

Mr Holt, the turnkey, soundlessly entered each cell and shook the prisoner by the shoulder. In those few minutes after waking each man was alone. The prospect of the day fell into place. Their time had come.

Within minutes their priests arrived – Canon Cantwell, Fr Quick and Fr Gadd – and reminded the men that priests in Manchester and Salford had implored their congregations to stay away from the execution and instead to gather in their parish churches. In churches throughout the land and across the sea in Ireland, men and women were gathering to offer the holy sacrifice of the Mass for them.

5.15 a.m.
They celebrated Mass in the tiny holding cell. The men knelt within touching distance of the altar, a scarred and rickety table. Candles burned steadily in two brass holders.

No draft disturbed them. The familiar smell of warm wax penetrated the staleness of the cell. The pristine whiteness of the altar linen was blinding against the flaking brick-work.

Fr Gadd's garments, vibrant green embroidered with threads of gold, were a warm presence in the chill cell. In that place of whispers and cowed words, the priest's voice was confident and warm. Solemnly he crossed himself: 'In nomine Patris, et Filii, et Spiritus Sancti. Amen.' The men followed his movements, crossing themselves with deliberation.

'Introibo ad altare Dei,' he intoned. 'I will go to the altar of God.'

'Ad deum qui laetificat juventutem meam,' they replied, 'To God, the giver of youth and happiness.'

They allowed the familiar words to wash over them, hypnotised by their cadences and the gestures of the priest as he performed the venerable ritual, a ritual and a faith that united them with each other and with generations of Irish men and women who had gone before them. They were caught up in the wonder of it, the recklessness of God's love. The priest raised the consecrated host above his head.

'Ecce Agnus Dei, ecce qui tollit peccata mundi,' intoned Fr Gadd, 'Behold the Lamb of God, behold Him who takes away the sins of the world.'

'Domine, non sum dignus, ut intres sub tectum meum: sed tantum dic verbo, et sanabitur anima mea,' came

O'Brien's response, 'Lord, I am not worthy to receive You; say but the word and I shall be healed.'

As Fr Gadd placed the host on Allen's tongue, he spoke the words, 'May the Body of Our Lord Jesus Christ keep thy soul unto life everlasting. Amen.'

6.00 A.M.

The sheriffs and their attendants arrived at the prison and went through the formalities of demanding that the condemned men be handed over to them. They then retired to the waiting room.

7.00 A.M.

As Fr Gadd and O'Brien finished folding the altar linen, the clock struck seven. From outside they heard the crowd shouting and hooting. They tried not to listen but the sound was as compelling as an overheard conversation.

A warder pushed open the door. Two orderlies carried in the trays of food – three platters, each with a wooden spoon, a jug of water and three wooden mugs. The turnkeys watched them from the doorway. They placed the contents of the trays on the table without raising their eyes.

'Thank you, gentlemen,' said Fr Gadd. At this one of the servers looked up and scanned the faces of the men. He had an impressive beard and a wall eye. The chalkiness of his deformed eye was striking in contrast to his black beard. 'Good luck,' he said. The server offered his hand. Larkin took it, then O'Brien and then Allen.

'Good luck to you all,' said the server. The turnkey said nothing, but beckoned him with a jerk of his head.

They set to with a will. The potatoes and gruel were tepid but the taste was wonderful: the earthiness of the potatoes, the glutinous tang of the grains and the coolness of the water.

7.03 A.M.

Calcraft stepped out onto the drop. His face was a chalky white, the same colour as his beard, and his head twitched like that of a palsied man. The fog, which reduced visibility to about thirty yards, obscured both ends of the street below: he could see only the space below the drop, cordoned off for the press. Before he checked the first noose, someone in the crowd spotted him.

'Look!' cried a pointing man, 'the grim reaper!'

Some laughed and others started up a hissing that increased in volume whenever he touched the ropes or gibbet.

'Bleedin' Old Father Time's here!' cried a woman from the crowd.

Some of the fifty or so reporters, gathered in the area directly in front of the scaffold reserved for them, smiled indulgently at the crowd and others looked up at the hangman. Some looked at their pocket watches and one called out to the executioner as he tested the rope with his weight, 'Everything secure, Cal? We don't want anyone to come to any harm.'

The old man made no reply, only patted his skullcap and wiped the palms of his hands on the lapels of his black suit. He moved to the second rope, followed by his impassive assistant, whose coat was open, displaying a vibrant and fashionable pink waistcoat.

'For Christ's sake do it right this time,' called up a top-hatted reporter, removing a cheroot from his mouth. 'We don't want to spend all day waiting for the poor buggers to croak.'

7.42 A.M.

From outside in the yard came the thunder of boots on the timber steps leading to the parapet. It was the sound of the 72nd Highlanders taking their position on the platform inside the prison walls. 'Take up positions,' came the command as the soldiers reached the top of the stairs. They knelt, crouching down behind the wall, now out of sight of the crowd in the streets below. The soldiers rested their rifles on the battlements and at the same time the heads and rifles of other soldiers appeared over the parapet of the railway bridge that ran at right angles to the prison wall.

At the foot of the stairs leading to the scaffold the prison warders on one side, with the 72nd Highlanders opposite them, formed a passageway for the condemned men.

7.45 A.M.

The men heard footfalls in the corridor outside the cell.

'Shall we prepare ourselves?' asked Fr Gadd.

The three men fell to their knees.

'Repeat this after me,' said the priest, raising his head from the book. 'Grant, we beseech Thee, O Lord, that in this, the hour of our death, we may be refreshed by Thy Holy Sacraments and delivered from all guilt, and so deserve to be received with joy into the arms of Thy mercy. Through Christ our Lord. Amen.

'Lord,' continued Fr Gadd.

'Have mercy on us,' came the reply.

'Christ …'

'Have mercy on us.'

'Lord God, the Father of heaven …'

'Have mercy on us.'

'God, the Son, Redeemer of the world …'

'Have mercy on us.'

'God, the Holy Ghost …'

'Have mercy on us.'

'Holy Trinity, one God …'

'Have mercy on us.'

'Jesus, Son of the living God …'

'Have mercy on us.'

'Jesus, Splendour of the Father …'

'Have mercy on us.'

'Jesus, Brightness of eternal light …'

'Have mercy on us.'

'Jesus, most amiable …'

'Have mercy on us.'

'Jesus, Father of the world to come …'

'Have mercy on us.'

'Jesus, most powerful …'

'Have mercy on us.'

'Jesus, most patient …'

'Have mercy on us.'

'Jesus, Lover of us …'

'Have mercy on us.'

'Jesus, Author of life …'

'Have mercy on us.'

'Jesus, our God …'

'Have mercy on us.'

'Jesus, our Refuge …'

'Deliver us.'

'From all evil …'

'Deliver us.'

'From all sin …'

'Deliver us.'

'From everlasting death …'

'Deliver us.'

'Through the mystery of Thy holy incarnation …'

'Deliver us.'

'Through Thy agony and passion …'

'Deliver us.'

'Through Thy pains and torments …'

'Deliver us.'

'Through Thy death and burial ...'

'Deliver us.'

'Through Thy resurrection ...'

'Deliver us.'

'Through Thy ascension ...'

'Deliver us.'

'Lamb of God who takest away the sins of the world ...'

'Spare us, O Jesus.'

Outside the cell Calcraft and Armstrong, the latter with his topcoat removed and his pink waistcoat fully visible, were busy preparing the harnesses to pinion the prisoners. Of all the things Calcraft had achieved during his long career as public executioner this was the thing he valued most. With his harness he could secure the prisoner quickly without the slightest discomfort and have him ready for execution in a matter of seconds.

'Mr Calcraft,' said the governor, who stood five paces along the corridor from the cell door. 'A word, sir.' He stood at his full height, arms clasped behind his back.

'Yes, sir.' Calcraft looped the harnesses around Armstrong's outstretched arm and then moved along the corridor. The governor bent his head to the executioner.

'Early this morning I received a telegram from the home secretary. Mr Gathorne-Hardy acknowledges your concerns and asks me to assure you that your personal safety and that of ...' he looked down the corridor towards Armstrong, 'your assistant, is guaranteed.'

'Thank you, sir,' said Calcraft, patting his skullcap.

'Much obliged, sir.'

Meanwhile the corridor was filling with silent officials. The governor cast his eye along the line. To the right of the door was the chief warder, his buttons gleaming against the dark blue of his uniform. Behind him, the prison chaplain, white surplice over his black cassock, his hands folded over his prayer book, gold, green and white tassels hanging from it. To the left stood the two lines of four warders. The two wand bearers, carrying the symbols of the ultimate sanction of the law, and the prison surgeon waited at the side, ready to take up their positions. They had an air of weary detachment, reluctant participants.

The clock struck the hour. Eight. Then the prison bell boomed and began to toll. The noise was painful in the corridor. It seemed that the great bell was just above them and the whole prison was a sounding board for its tolling.

Gong.

'Lord have mercy on us,' came the voices from inside the cell. The response was strong and firm.

Gong.

'Lord have mercy on us.'

'Most merciful Jesus, lover of souls, I pray Thee, by the agonies of Thy most Sacred Heart and by the sorrows of Thine Immaculate Mother, to wash in Thy most precious blood the sinners of the world who are now in their agony and who will die today. Heart of Jesus, once in agony, have mercy on those about to die. Amen.' The priest's voice was strong and even.

Gong.

The governor cradled his watch in the palm of his left hand and released the cover with his thumb. He nodded and the chief warder unlocked the cell. Calcraft and Armstrong stepped through the door.

'Excuse me, sir. Are you ready?' Though his question was addressed to Fr Gadd, it was the men who answered. They looked at Calcraft with surprise. Though everything that had happened to them since their conviction had spun in the orbit of this moment, now that it had arrived, they were taken by surprise.

'We are,' each said.

Calcraft offered his hand to O'Brien.

'Only my duty,' he said.

'Don't I know that,' said O'Brien taking his hand. 'No hard feelings.'

'Thank you, gentlemen,' said Calcraft as he fastened the final halter on Larkin. He indicated the doorway and Allen stepped out first, followed by Larkin, who was a ghastly white and unsteady on his feet, and then O'Brien. Allen was holding a small wooden cross.

Fr Gadd immediately took up the litany.

'Jesus, King of glory ...'

'Have mercy on us,' came the chorused reply. O'Brien's voice was firm and resolute, Allen's quavering and Larkin's faint. The bell continued to toll. As the procession made its way through corridors, through open doors and then out into the yard, the men continued to respond. The damp air prickled their skin and so heightened was their awareness that it felt like sandpaper drawn across their faces and hands. Two lines of warders formed a corridor from the entrance of the yard to the foot of the stairs leading to the scaffold. Every warder looked straight ahead into the face of the man opposite.

The small procession reached the foot of the stairs. The tolling of the bell stopped. Allen, with Canon Cantwell at his side, halted and taking an audible breath began the ascent. The smell of white pine filled his head. The only sound was that of Fr Gadd's voice and the men's responses. At the top of the steps they stopped behind the door to the drop which hid them from the public.

Calcraft pushed open the door. Allen saw the noose. Then he looked down into 1,000 upturned faces damp with mist. And though he could not clearly discern their features or see the expressions on their faces, the tilt of their heads and their stillness spoke of their awe. Then Allen snapped his head upwards.

'Jesus have mercy on us.'

Larkin staggered up the steps. As soon as he reached the top, Calcraft took Allen by the elbow and guided him through the door to the drop.

'Hats off,' came the cry from below and there was a great shuffling among the crowd, as the men removed their headwear.

Calcraft positioned Allen under the beam and slipped the bag over his head. He then placed the noose around his neck and drew it tight so the knot was under his left ear and his head was tilted to the right like a man with a ricked neck. Allen answered the litany, his voice now muffled.

'Trust in your saviour,' said Canon Cantwell.

Calcraft bent and secured Allen's feet and then, leaving him in the charge of a turnkey, returned to guide O'Brien to his position.

'Lord Jesus, have mercy on us,' said Allen, his voice faltering. 'Lord Jesus, receive my soul.' The bag over Allen's head was now plastered to his face with moisture, showing the outline of his nose and eye sockets.

As O'Brien was steered to his position under the noose, he turned to Allen and kissed him on his hooded forehead.

'God bless you, Willy.'

Calcraft hooded O'Brien, placed the noose around his neck and bound his feet.

When Larkin passed through the door and saw the others, he faltered like a man struck a heavy blow in the face. O'Brien turned his blind eyes to him.

'We're here, with you, Mikey,' said O'Brien.

Calcraft placed the bag over Larkin's head, covered it with the noose and tied his legs. Immediately he wilted. The two turnkeys held him upright by the elbows.

'Christ have mercy on us,' said O'Brien, his voice strong and clear.

Calcraft checked the nooses one last time. The priests withdrew from the drop, stooping under the gibbet and between the men.

An appalled silence fell over the crowd. The floor clattered from under the men and they fell out of sight.

10

'HOT AND BITTER TEARS'

Longsight Market, Manchester,
Sunday 22 November 1987

The flame devoured the orange corner of the flag. Then it leaped up the thin material and enveloped the Tricolour. The circle round the flag broke and danced back in a demented jig, their great boots slapping on the tarmac. Whooping, they held the flagpole above the heads of the line of policemen facing them so those across the road in the market could see it burning.

One of the flag-burners broke away and ran towards the cordon of police around the market.

'Get back,' said the policeman, from behind his visor. The skinhead stopped, looked at the policeman, retreated across the road and then levered himself up a lamp post with the agility of a tree surgeon.

'Murdering fucking Irish fucking bastards,' he bellowed. He stabbed his middle finger in the air. The November mizzle glazed his shorn head and in the grainy light his skull was as pale as a baby's skin.

'Fuck off back to your own country,' cried another flag-burner, his chest thrust out, his legs splayed. They were all dressed the same – boots laced up to the shin, skin-tight jeans, black bomber jackets and shaven heads. The lamp post-scaler, however, was distinctive: across his throat was a broken blue line and above it the legend *Cut Here*.

They burned another Tricolour, waving it above the heads of the policemen, gambolling like demons ecstatic at another soul plunging down to hell. 'Revenge for Enniskillen, revenge for Enniskillen, revenge for Enniskillen,' they chanted, pumping their boots on the ground.

Across the road in the market, the marchers watched impassively. Separating the two forces were hundreds of policemen, many mounted on nervous horses, which snorted and whinnied as they shuffled sideways. There were as many policemen as marchers.

In the market the loudhailer squealed. 'We need to form up now, guys,' came the command. The speaker was a youth of about twenty in a duffle coat and with a wisp of ginger beard. 'We're actually behind schedule, folks.'

Two marshals beckoned them into position. The flute band struck up 'Roddy McCorley', a tribute to the young United Irishman executed for his part in the rising of 1798, and they moved off at a self-conscious shuffle along the narrow lanes between the market stalls. The noise from behind the police cordon changed from a tattered screaming of abuse and hooting to a wail of strident whistles which drowned out the band.

***

The 1987 Manchester commemoration of the execution of Allen, Larkin and O'Brien – the Manchester Martyrs – was not the only event to demonstrate the contentiousness of their legacy. From the day they died people have fought over their memory and their meaning. Nationalists lauded them as courageous and self-sacrificing martyrs in the pursuit of the highest patriotic ideals, men whose story crystallises the grievances and justifies the struggle of those fighting for Irish independence: they were the victims of judicial murder, proof of Britain's intractable hatred of the Irish people. For these nationalists, the Martyrs immediately became a byword for everything that was brutal, unjust and cynical about British rule in Ireland.

Inevitably the executions brought thousands clamouring to the Fenian cause. John Devoy, in his memoir, summed up their significance when he wrote, 'No single act of the British authorities in the nineteenth century deepened the bitterness between Ireland and England more than the hanging of Allen, Larkin and O'Brien. And none served more in the strengthening of the Irish national ideal.' Marx's collaborator, Friedrich Engels, who lived in Manchester and was familiar with its Fenian tradition, also regarded the executions as a turning point. In his opinion they had 'accomplished the final act of separation between England

and Ireland. The only thing the Fenians had lacked were martyrs. They have been provided with these.'

The events which took place in Manchester in 1867 are as significant for the nineteenth-century development of Irish nationalism as those in Dublin in 1916 are for the twentieth.

Before the executions, actions in Ireland had conditioned the outlook and concerns of the Irish abroad. The events of 1867, however, though they took place outside Ireland, had a major impact on Irish nationalist politics and influenced the outlook of nationalists all over the world. *The Irish Catholic Chronicle* and *People's News of the Week* were in no doubt that 'a deed was done that has sundered Englishmen and Irishmen for this generation' and caused 'relations between the two countries to regress half a century'.

What's more the executions temporarily removed the greatest single obstacle to the progress of Fenianism, namely, the ambivalent attitude of the church to nationalism. They united the church with all shades of nationalist opinion. As Robert Kee, in his book *The Green Flag*, puts it, 'Men who resisted with their whole strength the Fenian movement – priests who denounced it from the altar – have shed hot and bitter tears over this deed of blood.' In fact, most people in Ireland heard of the executions at Mass the following day, Sunday 24 November, when their priests announced it from the pulpit. Contemporary accounts tell of spontaneous outpourings of grief. Many parish priests immediately scheduled Requiem Masses for the repose of the dead men's souls, thereby fusing Catholic and nationalist fervour. All over Britain enormous crowds turned up for demonstrations of solidarity with the executed men. In many places parishioners draped their churches in black for the occasion. So effusive were the clergy in sympathy for the Martyrs that Lord Mayo, chief secretary for Ireland, accused the priests of 'making mischief' and was particularly concerned that even Cardinal Cullen, Archbishop of Armagh, Primate of all Ireland and widely regarded as an enemy of nationalism, instructed priests in his diocese to offer Masses for the repose of the souls of the Martyrs.

On the other hand, those who demonstrated against the 1987 Manchester commemoration were neither the only, nor the first, to see in the Martyrs the embodiment of everything that is wrong with violence-condoning nationalists: murderers, destroyers of the peace, enemies of order and rightful authority, dangerous fanatics who have no place in a democratic society. *The Belfast Newsletter* perhaps summed up this attitude best when it described the executions as 'beyond all question just and imperative'. The whole affair was a 'miserable tragedy'. The *Newsletter* saw nothing of heroism or idealism, but lamented that 'three unhappy men have been sent to their account, victims to their own madness, and to the credulity with which they listened to agitators on the one side and conspirators on the other.'

For over a hundred years after the events, the commemorations continued to arouse powerful and conflicting feelings. To a large extent this is because, throughout its entire history, the commemoration has inevitably become associated with contemporary conflicts and the passions they arouse.

Further, the manner in which the British authorities handled the aftermath of the executions served only to compound the assault on Irish sensibilities. The government refused to release the bodies of the men for burial and insisted that they be interred within the confines of the prison in unconsecrated ground. This inflamed Irish indignation as it denied the men the Christian burial which is so important in Irish religious and cultural tradition. It was the subsequent decision of nationalists to enact funerals, even in the absence of the dead, which enabled them to circumvent the official ban on political demonstrations.

The intensity of feeling aroused by the commemorations is comparable to the outpouring of public grief which has marked the passing of those national figures who have come to symbolise a people's history: Queen Victoria, Winston Churchill, Franklin Roosevelt, Abdul Nasser, Michael Collins and Éamon de Valera are such people. These emotions united the Irish throughout the world. As one of the organisers of the Dublin commemoration of 1867 put it, 'There is probably no parallel in history for the singular circumstance of these processions being held by the dispersed Irish in lands remote ... in Europe, in

America, in Australia.' Each commemoration fused the participants in shared indignation and heightened patriotic ardour.

The first commemoration took place in Manchester on 24 November 1867, the day after the executions, when 10,000 marched through the streets in incessant rain, halting at the home of Allen's mother and that of Larkin's wife and mother. Many sobbed openly. The atmosphere was profoundly mournful, the focus on shared grief. Afterwards the sodden marchers dispersed in a manner so orderly that it met with the approval of *The Manchester Courier*, not noted for its sympathetic attitude to the Irish.

On Sunday 1 December a second Manchester demonstration took place. Contrary to the urgent pleas of the clergy, 15,000 marched the two miles from Stephenson Square to the site of the execution. The police were conspicuously absent and there was no trouble. The organisers printed cards commemorating the execution in green ink. On the same day thousands turned out for commemorations in Limerick city and at four places in Michael O'Brien's native County Cork – Cork city, Mitchelstown, Skibbereen and Midleton.

The demonstration in Cork city was one of the biggest. It took what was already the established format of a funeral procession with the mourners wearing crêpe bands tied with green ribbons. As a mark of solidarity with the marchers all public houses were closed and virtually every Mass-goer that Sunday wore some emblem of mourning.

Each of the three hearses, drawn by six horses, carried a coffin with the name of one of the martyrs inscribed in black on white linen. Three carriages followed them – the first with Allen's mother, the second empty and the third with O'Brien's brother and his sister-in-law.

The Birmingham demonstration attracted several thousand mourners. Even the unsympathetic press was impressed by the religious fervour of the crowd, who knelt to pray for the dead men. The London demonstration started from Clerkenwell Green and included a funeral oration. Pleading that counter-demonstrations might lead to violent disorder, the government banned commemorative funerals planned for Glasgow, Newcastle, Liverpool, Warrington, Davenport, Plymouth, Bolton, Sunderland, Rochester, Lichfield and Wolverhampton.

The Dublin funeral of 8 December was the most impressive in Ireland and the British Isles. Despite relentless sleet, 60,000 took part, all wearing green ribbons or an item of green clothing. The procession took one hour and forty minutes to pass the Four Courts en route to Glasnevin Cemetery where John Martin, a veteran of the 1848 rising, delivered the oration as chairman of the funeral committee. Martin bought a burial plot in Glasnevin Cemetery in readiness for the bodies of the executed men, which became the focus of both the first and subsequent commemorations in the city. In his speech he uttered sentiments that were later deemed seditious and landed him, and others involved in the demonstration, in prison. What particularly upset the authorities was his mention of 'legal murder' and his description of the executed as 'pious men who feared God and loved their country'. He and John Walters, a leading Fenian, orchestrated a campaign to raise money on behalf of the Martyrs' families. Significantly, John McHale, the Archbishop of Tuam, opened one list.

The Dublin commemoration was for a number of years in the early 1870s linked to the Amnesty Association campaign for the release of Fenian prisoners, and remained an extremely important event in the nationalist calendar.

For their part the British government seemed determined to ensure that the Fenians squeezed the maximum propaganda advantage from the commemorations. The decision to prosecute a number of the Dublin organisers was a political disaster. The most famous of these were John Martin and A. M. Sullivan, whose eloquence before the court ensured their status as nationalist heroes and victims of British oppression. However, it was Sullivan's brother, Timothy Daniel Sullivan, who produced the most enduring monument to the Martyrs. Immediately after the executions he took up Edward Condon's speech from the dock and used it in his song, 'God Save Ireland', which was sung to the tune of 'Tramp! Tramp! Tramp!' the American Civil War marching song or 'The Prisoner's Hope'.[3] It immediately became popular and was at once taken up as Ireland's unofficial national anthem, sung at every patriotic

---

3   See Appendix 2.

gathering for forty years, until 'A Soldiers' Song' superseded it. 'God Save Ireland' has endured in popularity, greatly enhanced by John McCormack whose 1910 recording did most to introduce it to a new generation.

Of less importance, but nevertheless significant, was a joint enterprise by the Sullivan brothers: the publication in 1868 of the popular *Speeches from the Dock*, much of it devoted to the Manchester men. Later the Sullivans' 'Dying Declarations of the Manchester Victims' cemented the position of the Martyrs' place in nationalist iconography.

The organisers of the Dublin commemoration were not the only ones made to face the courts. When news of the executions reached Hokatika, New Zealand, early in 1868 the significant Irish community in the area immediately assembled to register their outrage. Fr Larkin and the editor of the *Hokatika Celt*, William Manning, were later arrested and convicted for their role in organising the protest. The Irish of nearby Charleston set up a relief fund committee and a commemorative funeral attended by over a thousand people heard Fr Hallam, a local priest, describe the events surrounding the executions as surpassing anything that a writer of fiction could concoct.

***

Events in London in December 1867 transformed the significance of commemoration of the Martyrs in an instant. On 13 December Ricard O'Sullivan Burke, the Fenian armaments organiser, was remanded to Clerkenwell

Prison. In a botched rescue bid, involving an enormous quantity of explosives, a large section of the prison wall was demolished, a number of houses totally destroyed and many others badly damaged. Far more significant was the killing of twelve innocent Londoners and the maiming of over a hundred more.

Karl Marx, who was living in London at the time, summed up the significance of this event: 'The London masses, who have shown great sympathy towards Ireland, will be made wild and driven into the arms of a reactionary government. One cannot expect the London proletarians to allow themselves to be blown up in honour of Fenian emissaries.'

All over the country, the police swore in special constables to guard against the Fenian menace, 5,000 in the city of London alone. The Irish problem was no longer a peripheral concern. It had intruded into the heart of English life.

The short period between the executions and the Clerkenwell explosion marked the pinnacle of Fenianism. Never again would it enjoy such public sympathy; never again would it be able to present itself in such a favourable light and draw upon such a wealth of patriotic and religious fervour. Indeed, the executions demonstrated the strengths of Fenianism – the audacity, courage, selflessness and passion of Irishmen 'of no property'. But they also demonstrated its weaknesses, for it was only when the movement drew on wider political, social and economic concerns, particularly land ownership, that it was able to transform this sympathy into widespread support among the Irish population. The organisation subsequently dissipated the goodwill it had accrued in acts of senseless destruction and a further futile campaign to acquire territory in Canada. It soon became clear that it was also at odds with Catholic teaching and the papacy's position on political violence. In 1870 the church, in condemning the Fenians as an oath-bound secret society, made its official position clear and forbad Catholics to join, under pain of sin. Though many chose to disregard the warning – including a number of parish priests and curates – this censure was nevertheless a serious blow to the organisation in a country then noted for its intense religious feeling and the power of the church hierarchy.

The events of 1867 did have a number of long-term effects. They catapulted Ireland to the top of the British political agenda. They certainly had a profound effect on Gladstone, who set himself the task of resolving the Irish situation, and other leading figures of the last decades of the nineteenth century, such as Isaac Butt, who founded a political party committed to winning Home Rule for Ireland by democratic means. Charles Stewart Parnell steered it so successfully that he became 'Ireland's uncrowned king'. The Home Rule Party had almost achieved its goal and won an Irish parliament – albeit with limited powers – when the outbreak of the Great War in August 1914 led to the suspension of its implementation.

Further afield reaction to the executions was uniformly negative, even among traditionally pro-British groups. The *New York Herald*, for instance, warned that the British government had lost international sympathy for her 'domestic troubles'. Cities such as New York and Chicago, with their large Irish populations, quickly developed a tradition of commemoration that became an established part of the life of the Irish community. It soon became customary to combine the commemoration with concerts and lectures. Many of the commemoration venues were prestigious. In 1902, for instance, Madison Square Garden hosted the event.

The Clerkenwell explosion had little impact in the many Irish towns and cities where torchlight processions were a common feature of the commemoration. Control of the organisation of these events, however, soon became problematic. Various groups sought to appropriate the occasion and manipulate it for their own political ends. Initially it was the Fenians who held sway, but as the century wore on and the Land League became a key factor in Irish politics, great numbers of constitutional nationalists became keen to partake in the commemorations. In Dublin, however, the Fenians maintained their grip on proceedings to a far greater extent than in provincial Ireland.

Outside the capital commemorations sometimes became the focus of hostility between nationalists and the authorities. The Enniscorthy commemoration of 27 November 1890, for instance, ended in disarray when police charged the crowd and inflicted several injuries.

A great deal of the veneration of the Martyrs manifested itself in many Irish communities in the building of permanent memorials. In Manchester a public subscription paid for a monument erected in the republican plot of St Joseph's Cemetery, Moston, the first Catholic burial ground in the city and the last resting place of countless paupers who escaped the Famine only to die shortly after arriving. Commissioned by the Manchester Martyrs Central Memorial Committee, founded in 1898, it stands just over twenty feet high and takes the form of a Celtic Cross. With medallion portraits of the three men,

The Martyrs'
memorial,
St Joseph's
Cemetery
Courtesy
of Mercier
Archives

it stands on a base of granite from the Hill of Tara and contains the figures of Unity, Justice, Literature and Art on the corners. Predictably the monument became a focus for the intense nationalist feeling of those Irish people living in the area.

The ceremony of laying the foundation stone, carried out by James Stephens – no longer regarded as a threat by the authorities – drew enormous crowds. Afterwards Stephens and Maude Gonne spoke. In 1909 Condon himself, who had been released from jail in 1878 and exiled to America, and was by this time a constitutional nationalist, visited the memorial.

At about this time numerous other memorials were erected all over Ireland. One of the most impressive stands in the centre of Kilrush, County Clare. The inscription tells us it was erected in 1903 by a committee of Kilrush nationalists through 'public subscriptions received from Irishmen the world over'. Many of the monuments, such as those in Birr, County Offaly and in Tipperary town, became prominent landmarks. The latter was commonly known as 'The Maid of Erin' and was erected in 1907, an occasion marked by a mass demonstration of Fenian sympathy.

By the end of the nineteenth century the traditional format of the Manchester commemoration was well established. It was customary for marchers to wear cockades of the Fenian colours, green and black. The procession, usually headed by the North East Manchester

Reed Band, formed up in Bexley Square, Salford, near the execution site. Their route took the marchers past where the Martyrs died to eleven o'clock Mass at St Patrick's, Livesey Street, the church which served Manchester's oldest Irish settlement, Irish Town, for over a century. After Mass the procession marched down Rochdale Road, the centre of Irish Manchester, and then back to the parish centre for a public meeting.

During this period and in the years immediately before the Great War, the Home Rule agitation for an Irish parliament with responsibility for many aspects of her affairs was steadily gathering momentum. In 1914 a bill establishing this parliament was imminent. The opposition of unionists – mainly Irish Protestants – who were threatening to take military action to prevent Home Rule, was all that stood between Ireland and independence. At this time large commemorative gatherings were held in Manchester and Cork and it was common for speakers to paraphrase the words of John Mitchel, advising those without guns to sell their clothes to get them. However, the outbreak of the Great War in 1914 – which led to the suspension of Home Rule for the duration – postponed the crisis.

After the Great War the Martyrs assumed a new significance as they became the focus for anti-British feelings in the aftermath of the 1916 Easter Rising and preamble to the War of Independence. In 1919 the Cork commemorations went ahead in defiance of a government ban and those assembling for the march were dispersed by British soldiers threatening to fire on them with a machine gun.

In the inter-war period, with the establishment of the Irish Free State, the emphasis of the commemorations changed. For many, the Irish independence for which the Martyrs gave their lives had become a reality. For others, however, it remained a distant dream, betrayed by those who'd settled for a Free State which left six counties under British rule.

During this period the Gaelic League played a prominent role in the Manchester Commemorative Committee. The traditional march and public meeting were still the focal point of the commemoration but a new element was introduced. It now became customary for a group to march from the Ben Brierley pub, a local meeting place on Moston Lane, to the monument in St Joseph's Cemetery, known locally as Moston cemetery, where they said a decade of the Rosary. From there they walked the few yards to the grave of Seán Morgan, a republican shot by the police in 1921, where they again prayed. Once more the link between religious and nationalist sentiment was affirmed.

In the years immediately after the Second World War the commemoration was still going strong. In 1947 it involved benediction at the cemetery chapel and a ceilidh at the Tara Club, Queen's Road, a popular venue for the city's large and vibrant Irish community constantly replenished by the enormous post-war influx of immigrants.

The guest of honour at the 1949 commemoration was Éamon de Valera, then in opposition, who addressed a rally at the King's Hall, Belle Vue, not far from the spot where Kelly and Deasy were rescued. This was a time when a new, more assured nationalism was emerging, with the unification of Ireland as its chief objective. The Anti-Partition of Ireland League was at the height of its popularity with the Irish in England. The Terence MacSwiney Pipe Band played 'God Save Ireland' and 'A Nation Once Again'.

The programme for that evening gives a flavour of the sentiments expressed:

> The position in Northern Ireland must not be allowed to continue. Let us show the world, and especially the English-speaking world, what an evil thing it is that we are fighting: the abrogation of common law, imprisonment without charge, without redress; democracy flouted, elections gerrymandered, and all the other repression that goes to make a totalitarian state. This puppet state is under the British flag and supported by British finance, and it would seem that England is prepared to support any corruption, any graft, and any persecution to hold on to the north of Ireland.

Despite the presence of de Valera at the 1949 commemoration, the scale of the event began to wane in the early 1950s. According to the *Irish Democrat*, the organising committee was the cause of the decline, treating the commemoration as its own private property instead of the possession of the Irish people. The event had all but died out when, in 1954, Seamus Barrett, the noted Manchester republican, revived it. For a while, the profile of the commemoration was restored and it was second only to Easter in the nationalist calendar. But this was merely a temporary respite in what appeared to be terminal decline.

The disunity within the Irish community that blighted these years came to the fore in 1954, when attendance at the commemoration was the largest for a number of years. The organising committee and the Connolly Association were at odds and the latter's wreath was destroyed in the cemetery.

Discord was such that in the following years there were three separate commemorations, none of which was well attended. The committee's decision to ban wreaths upset many who had once formed the mainstay of the event. Several of the old Lancashire Irish Associations boycotted the commemoration. There were claims that the exclusiveness and intransigence of the organisers were driving people away.

The Manchester Martyrs Commemoration Committee leaflet of 1957 sought to clarify its purpose. The march, it said, was 'in honour of the soldiery of every generation who died for the indestructible cause of the Irish Republic'. The Connolly Association turned out in force that year but the total attendance was described as 'very poor'.

In 1958 a speaker from the organising committee complained of the poor turnout from among the Manchester

Irish and said that if it had not been for those from London, Warrington and Birmingham 'we should have presented a very sorry spectacle here today'. The commemoration took the form of a protest against the sentences imposed on Kevin Mallon and Patrick Talbot the previous year in Belfast and demanded the withdrawal of British troops from Ireland. Both speakers were from the Connolly Association.

At about this time an open letter in the *Irish Democrat* criticised the commemoration committee, calling it the monopoly of a single group with narrow views which refused to cooperate with others. The committee had fallen out with the Gaelic League and the Anti-Partition League and repeatedly rebuffed advances from the Connolly Association and Sinn Féin. They had abolished the tradition of each association presenting a wreath. Yet, under Barrett's influence, all organisations which stood for the ending of British rule in Ireland had taken part in the commemoration.

In 1959 the commemoration was held at the arch where Kelly and Deasy were rescued, one of only two places where a plaque, erected in 1988, marks the contribution of the Irish to the history of the city. Throughout this decade the Connolly Association held an Irish week to precede the Manchester Martyrs Commemoration. Executive members of the Irish Anti-Partition League were prominent.

In the early 1960s the focus of the commemoration moved to Platt Fields, a large municipal park near what was by then a major centre of the city's Irish population. In 1963, C. Desmond Greaves, editor of the *Irish Democrat*, and the Manchester leader of the Allied Engineering Union, addressed those gathered for the commemoration. It was at this commemoration that the civil rights issue in Northern Ireland was first raised.

As the centenary of the executions approached the Manchester Connolly Association began planning the construction of a monument on the site of the New Bailey, the place of execution. When the prison was demolished in 1868, the site became a railway goods yard beside Salford Station. In 1967 *The Manchester Evening News* and *The Manchester Guardian* offices were in construction on the spot where the executions took place.

The sculptor Arthur Dooley, known to the public chiefly because of his controversial *Stations of the Cross* in a Catholic church in Leyland, Lancashire, accepted the commission to design the new monument. Mr Redmond, chairman of the Connolly Association, opened a public subscription and a number of prominent personalities, including two Labour MPs – Stan Orme and Paul Rose – and Alderman Lesley Lever, made donations.

When Dooley and Redmond went to Ireland to select the five-tonne granite stone base they created a great stir. Radio Éireann interviewed them and Telefís Éireann made a film of their progress. Eventually, they found their rock in County Wicklow.

The project was well advanced: shipment of the stone

was imminent and Kathleen Clarke, the widow of Tom Clarke, one of the leaders of the 1916 Easter Rising, agreed to unveil the monument. At this stage the proposal was for a monument in Stanley Street. Then the Salford City engineer and surveyor announced that planning permission was needed.

Redmond applied for permission to build the memorial instead in Aldine House forecourt or Bailey Yard, Salford. It was refused on the grounds that it was 'out of keeping with the character of the area'. Redmond succeeded in getting the matter referred to the full council, who by twenty-eight to twenty-four, instructed the planning committee to reconsider. They did – then issued another rejection. The purpose of the commemorative rally of 26 November 1967 was to put pressure on the council. But it did not end there. The issue was debated at the highest level. A TD (member of the lower house of the parliament of Ireland, Dáil Éireann) questioned the Republic's Minister for External Affairs in the Dáil, asking him to intercede with the British government to secure a site for the monument. But in reality, the project was dead.

Redmond believed that it was the police and the management of *The Manchester Evening News* who killed it. As for the five tonnes of Wicklow rock, it simply disappeared.

The nature of the commemorations also underwent a fundamental change at this time. The slum-clearance programme obliterated the traditional Irish areas of the cities of Manchester and Salford, the streets where the Martyrs had lived and worked. The community was scattered and more upwardly mobile and the format and focus of the commemoration changed radically. But it was more the development of the civil rights campaign in Northern Ireland than changes in Manchester that brought this about.

Before 1973 the commemorations attracted little or no publicity. The attitude of *The Manchester Evening News* had always been one of studied indifference. This was only possible so long as the organising committee consisted largely of moderate constitutional nationalists. Their political outlook was demonstrated by their invitation to John Hume to be guest of honour. But in the early 1970s some elements sympathetic to armed struggle came to dominate and when violence in Northern Ireland escalated the commemoration became the focus of intense controversy.

Máire Drumm, vice-president of Sinn Féin, gave the oration in 1973. The newspapers talked of 'an IRA-style march in an English city'. As the time for the 1974 commemoration approached the press campaign for an official ban escalated and the Catholic Bishop of Salford, Thomas Holland, announced that the march would not be allowed to enter the cemetery. In 1967 he had celebrated High Mass to commemorate the centenary of the Martyrs' execution.

Developments in Northern Ireland again forced the Irish

issue to the forefront of British politics. Not surprisingly, in Manchester the Irish Civil Rights Association was involved in the organisation of the forthcoming commemoration. An Irishman, Neil Boyle, unsuccessfully stood for election as MP for Moss Side, an inner-city area with a large Irish population. He was against internment and sought to mobilise the Irish vote to influence British policy on Ireland.

In February 1974 a family local to Moston Cemetery – Lance Corporal Clifford Haughton, his wife, Linda, and their children Lee, five, and Robert, two – were killed in the M62 bombing. *The Manchester Evening News* reported a local shopkeeper who recalled marchers from the previous year in 'Provo uniform'. He said, 'there are a lot of rumours that there is a branch of the IRA in Moston'.

An Easter Sunday march to the Martyrs' monument was planned for 1974. When this became known the MP for Bury and Radcliffe, Mr Fidler, asked the Home Secretary to impose a ban. *The Manchester Evening News* reminded readers of the death of the Haughton family and stated that at the commemoration the previous November 'people who supported violence had used it as a platform'.

Predictably the march of Sunday 15 April 1974 was marked by violence and arrests. About a hundred marchers were confronted by 300 counter-demonstrators on Moston Lane, the approach to Moston Cemetery. A large number of local residents antagonistic to the march turned out to express their opposition. When the marchers reached the cemetery, they found the gates locked against them. An attempt to hold a memorial at the entrance was defeated by the counter-demonstrators, who shouted them down. The sight of berets and dark glasses, which had come to be seen by British TV audiences as the attire of terrorists, angered many of the locals.

The following month two men from Liverpool were convicted of behaviour likely to cause a breach of the peace and fined £25 each for their part in the disturbance at the cemetery gates. In their defence it was said they were incensed by marchers carrying the Tricolour, and wearing berets and dark glasses. The fines of the convicted were partly defrayed by the staff of a north Manchester engineering firm, who collected £7 on their behalf.

In the weeks immediately before the 1974 November commemoration, two Moston councillors sought to have the march banned. Rev. Paul Newberry, also from Moston, told the local papers that the march was 'not Christian – it's an abomination'. The police took seriously a number of threats to blow up the monument, to the extent that two constables spent a couple of long nights in the cemetery guarding it. The Birmingham bombing took place the week before the scheduled date of the commemoration and the organisers called off the march.

Nevertheless, 250 counter-demonstrators, National Front and loyalist, turned out 'just in case'. Kingsley Reid, the chairman of the National Front, was there and for two hours they chanted anti-Catholic and loyalist songs.

For seven years thereafter there were small commemorations at the monument. The earlier tradition of laying a wreath was revived and the accompanying press releases stressed the democratic republican aspirations of those present. In 1976, for instance, a wreath was laid and a speaker from the Bogside, Derry, which was at the time regarded by many nationalists as the epicentre of struggle in Northern Ireland, addressed the assembly.

It was at this time that opponents of the commemoration vandalised the monument, smashing part of the masonry around the periphery and daubing the main structure, including the head of Christ, with black paint.

In 1977 the Easter commemoration at the monument was interrupted when police moved off the few dozen people who had gathered for the event. The following year the organising committee called off the commemoration, citing among their reasons 'the harassment of members and anti-Irish feeling generally in Manchester'. Instead a 'private, simple ceremony' was held. This was the pattern for three years.

Events in 1981 once more impinged on the Manchester commemoration. With the end of the hunger strikes the Manchester Hunger Strike committee re-formed the Manchester Martyrs Commemoration Committee and the marches were reintroduced. Requests that the City Council restore the monument met with no success.

The prelude to the first of the new era of marches was inauspicious. *The Manchester Evening News* billed it as a Sinn Féin demonstration. The paper described the

Manchester Martyrs as 'three IRA gunmen' hanged for the 'murder of an English police sergeant'. It informed its readers that a monument to the 'killers' was in the 'Catholic cemetery'.

About 300 people, including two flute bands from Glasgow and contingents from Birmingham, Nottingham and Yorkshire, gathered at St Patrick's, Livesey Street, for the first march since 1974. It was organised by the Manchester-based Sinn Féin cumann – the women's branch.

As in 1974, the bishop locked the cemetery gates. The marchers went instead to the Fenian Arch where wreaths were laid. The pattern for the 1980s was established. Eleven affiliated groups identified with the march and its purpose – 'solidarity with today's freedom fighters'. During the 1980s the leaflets advertising the march explicitly expressed their support for the armed struggle in Northern Ireland and linked the Martyrs to that tradition. The speakers at this time, such as Jim McAllister, Sinn Féin abstentionist member of the Northern Ireland Assembly, were often nationalist politicians from Northern Ireland or aligned with them.

The bishop's decision to close the cemetery gates shifted the commemoration away from the monument. In 1982 Alexandra Park was the assembly point for about 200 people. In what was to become a regular occurrence, the National Front held a counter-march. At this time Irish republican prisoners were one focus of nationalist political

activity and the organising committee's leaflet stated that
the march was in solidarity with them. At the time there
were fifty-two Irish political prisoners in British gaols,
including Strangeways, Manchester. The march was also
associated with the Viraj Mendis Defence Campaign
which was fighting against his deportation. The customary
National Front counter-demonstration took place and
there were ten arrests. The *Manchester Evening News*
coverage described it as a pro-IRA march and stated that
it was 'attended by 250 Sinn Féin members from various
parts of Britain'.

It was clear by 1985 that the nature of the commemoration had changed since the mid-1960s. It was no longer
exclusively, or even mainly, an Irish event, supported by
those who wished to honour Ireland's martyrs and thereby
express their patriotism. The supporters of the march were
now almost exclusively left-wingers who viewed the conflict in Northern Ireland as part of a wider class struggle.

Five hundred marchers, including contingents from
Birmingham, Edinburgh, Glasgow, Leeds, London and
Sheffield, took part in the 1985 event. A former internee
spoke, welcoming the support of the Irish in Britain
Representation Group, the Irish Republican Socialist
Party, The Pakistani Workers Association (Britain), The
Asian Youth Movement, The Troops Out Movement,
The Revolutionary Communist League, Fight Racism,
Fight Imperialism and the Irish Freedom Movement.
Other speakers drew parallels between the Martyrs and

political prisoners in Northern Ireland, the coal miners – then waging a protracted strike against the Conservative government's programme of pit closures – immigrants and the armed struggle. *Class Struggle*, which described itself as the newspaper of the party 'of Socialism and Liberation', reported the event.

However, approval was not the universal response. It is significant that some members of the Irish community canvassed support in the press for moving the memorial in Moston Cemetery to the Irish World Heritage Centre, Cheetham Hill, thereby reclaiming both the Martyrs and their commemoration for the Irish community. This also seemed justified for entirely pragmatic reasons, as media coverage of the commemorations attracted a great deal of adverse opinion and there was a real fear that the damage inflicted on the monument in the 1970s would be compounded.

Yet despite these concerns about the format and nature of the commemoration, the 1986 event was one of the most impressive for many years. The police estimated an attendance of 1,500 from all over the country, including eight bands from Scotland. The marchers assembled at Longsight Market in heavy rain and went through the wet streets to an indoor rally at Manchester University's Students' Union. About a hundred counter-demonstrators, the usual mix of National Front and Northern Ireland loyalists, kept up attacks on the march. Five of them found their way into custody. The main speakers were from the

Irish Republican Socialist Party and the Pan-African Congress.

Again in 1987 the march attracted a great deal of hostile press coverage. The Enniskillen bombing aroused considerable anti-Irish feeling and the local press implied that the marchers were sympathetic to those responsible for the atrocity. *The Manchester Evening News* published a number of letters expressing dismay at the proposed march, demanding a ban. D. Delaney, the press officer for the Manchester Martyrs Commemoration Committee, fuelled antagonism by publishing a letter in which he stated that the marchers supported armed struggle.

Manchester's chief constable, James Anderton, predicted that a 1,000-strong counter-demonstration would pose a threat to public order. At his request the march was banned, but a rally at Longsight Market, in the centre of an Irish area of the city, was allowed. There was a powerful police presence of 500 officers, 200 on horseback. About 500 took part in the commemoration, confronted by eighty National Front and loyalist demonstrators, who burned several Tricolours.

Anthony O'Connor's letter in *The Manchester Evening News* that November claimed that the commemoration had been highjacked by fringe political groups from Manchester, Glasgow and London and that the Manchester Irish community shunned it. Sinn Féin also had reservations. 'We believe the slogans and demands of this commemoration restrict its appeal', its press release stated, expressing its disquiet that the Martyrs were being relegated to minor figures in the struggle against international capitalism. They withdrew from the commemoration because they believed that it should emphasise the demand for British withdrawal and self-determination for the Irish people.

The controversy surrounding the commemoration had at least one beneficial effect: it aroused interest in the Martyrs' story and in 1987 Manchester City Council erected a commemorative plaque at the Fenian Arch, on Hyde Road, the spot where the rescue of Kelly and Deasy took place.

In 1988 the police once more outnumbered the 250 marchers as they assembled at Longsight Market and marched a square route past Manchester University and down Stockport Road back to the market. A number of left-wing groups and Viraj Mendis campaigners took part and brandished banners.

The Manchester Evening News coverage was again hostile. The marchers were described as a pro-IRA group commemorating men who had murdered a policeman. Three counter-demonstrators were arrested.

Longsight Market was again the assembly point in 1989. The attendance, estimated at over 1,000, was far more than the previous year and included the Brendan Convey Flute Band from Derry, supporters of the Birmingham Six and members of the Pakistani Workers' Association. It ended with a public meeting at the Pakistani Community Centre. Sinn Féin sent a message linking the commemoration to the Guildford Four injustice.

By this time the commemoration had become an established object of hostile media coverage – the days when the local press ignored it were long gone. The authorities' attitude of indifference had also changed: members of the commemoration committee claimed that they were the victims of official harassment. In June 1988 Michael Quinn from Canada became the sixth guest of the committee to be held under the Prevention of Terrorism Act. Quinn was a member of the St Peter's Social Justice Committee of Saskatchewan which had been on a fact-finding tour of Northern Ireland.

There were also increasing numbers in the Irish community anxious to distance themselves from the current focus of the commemoration, which they believed had moved away from its original purpose. The *Irish Post* claimed that the committee was in the hands of British left-wing groups and the case of Peter Weatherby suggests that there was some truth in this. Weatherby, a member of the commemoration committee, achieved brief national prominence when Nicholas Winterton, Conservative MP for Macclesfield, a town to the south of Manchester, tabled a question for Treasury Minister, Peter Lilley, suggesting that Weatherby's political activities were not consistent with his employment as a civil servant. Lilley informed the House that Weatherby's role in the Troops Out Movement was the subject of an internal civil service investigation. Press coverage linked Weatherby to the anti-Poll Tax demonstrations, protests against the Prevention of

Terrorism Act and activities in support of the Birmingham Six and republican prisoners. Despite Mr Winterton's disquiet, the government found no reason to sack Mr Weatherby.

Despite all the adverse publicity, there was no disturbance at the 1990 commemoration, and about 1,000 marched unmolested. As well as the Brendan Convey Flute Band from Derry, the Northern Ireland contingent provided a hundred-yard banner demanding the withdrawal of British troops from Northern Ireland. The commemoration committee linked the march to support for republican prisoners and the Birmingham Six Campaign, the Pakistani Workers Association and the Irish Republican Socialist Party. Supporters of Sharon and Michael Nelson, a local couple fighting against deportation, also took part. Many of the speakers at the 1991 event focused on the Birmingham Six.

In 1992 it was obvious from the pre-march publicity that the organisers were anxious to play down support for the armed struggle. At the meeting in Platt Fields there were three republican flute bands and twenty stewards from Glasgow, yet only 200 attended and only about thirty of these were from Manchester. Among them were Fr Des Wilson and members of The Irish in Britain Representation Group, the Black People's Alliance and the Pakistani Workers' Association. The decline in support for the event was, in the view of many observers, the result of the organisers' alienating much of city's long-established

Irish community by linking the commemorations to causes and individuals who enjoyed little sympathy.

In recent years, with the signing of the Good Friday Agreement and the end of inter-communal violence in Northern Ireland, interest in the Martyrs has revived. Members of the Irish community have cleaned and restored the monument in Moston Cemetery and beyond Manchester a revival of the tradition of commemoration is taking place in several areas where it was once an annual rite of nationalist commitment. In County Cork, Bandon's Annual Manchester Martyrs Commemoration Weekend is now a fixture in the local calendar. The annual commemoration at Hugginstown, South Kilkenny, attracts people from all over Ireland and that in Rath Cemetery, Tralee, County Kerry, is growing in popularity.

Much of this revival in the Republic of Ireland is associated with the rise of Sinn Féin as a force in democratic politics and its attempt to appropriate the country's republican heritage by playing a leading role in the commemoration of armed-struggle republicans from Wolfe Tone to the hunger strikers. Other parties, particularly Fianna Fáil, have long laid claim to the rebel tradition associated with the foundation of the state and are loath to relinquish it. Consequently, in order to reinforce their claim as the inheritors of the authentic national spirit, they have become more closely associated with commemorations of republican and Fenian figures.

All those involved in maintaining the memory of the

Martyrs agree that they provide a link between the United Irishmen of 1798 and the men of 1916, demonstrating the existence of an unbroken tradition of struggle for national independence. It is well known that of the men of 1916 Patrick Pearse and Tom Clarke were Fenians, consciously acting in a tradition they espoused. But the most celebrated link between the Fenian tradition and the events which led to the establishment of the Irish state occurred in 1915. That year the men who were to rise in rebellion in 1916 sought to use the funeral of the old Fenian Jeremiah O'Donovan Rossa, just as Stephens had used that of Terence Bellew McManus. Standing over his grave, Pearse invoked the tradition which O'Donovan Rossa had come to embody:

> They think that they have pacified Ireland. They think that they have purchased half of us and intimidated the other half. They think that they have foreseen everything, think that they have provided against everything; but the fools, the fools, the fools! – they have left us our Fenian dead, and while Ireland holds these graves, Ireland unfree shall never be at peace.

But there is a real sense in which the men of 1916 were inspired not only by O'Donovan Rossa, but by those whose empty grave lies only a few yards from his. For when the Rising for which they had planned for so long eventually arrived that Easter day, the leaders knew they had no prospect of achieving a military victory. Yet Pearse succeeded in convincing them that they should go ahead even though they knew it would end in their death. In effect they were making a blood sacrifice in the hope that it would once more unite the Irish nation just as it had been united for a short time after the execution of the Manchester Martyrs. This, they correctly surmised, would prove a first step to Ireland's freedom.

It was always anticipated that the Martyrs would eventually be buried in the grave prepared for them in Glasnevin. This hope, combined with political developments in the Republic during the early years of this century, resulted in the Irish government's decision to bring the Martyrs home and honour them with a state funeral. However, before this could be done, the bodies had to be located.

Like so much else about the Martyrs, their mortal remains provoked controversy. In Catholic and nationalist tradition the remains of martyrs are venerated. By consigning the Manchester Martyrs' bodies to quicklime in unconsecrated ground within the gaol the authorities, as one contemporary put it, 'branded their inanimate bodies with infamy'. For many years the whereabouts of their remains was shrouded in mystery. During 1868, when the New Bailey was closed, its prisoners were transferred to Manchester's new penal establishment, Strangeways, now known as Manchester (HM Prison) and the site of the old prison became a railway goods yard. Almost from the beginning, there was uncertainty about what had happened to the remains of the Martyrs and the three common criminals who were also executed at the New Bailey, all of whom had been buried within the confines of the place of execution.

This uncertainty arose partly because of various rumours circulating at different times and because for over a century the authorities remained silent on the matter. The rumours suggested that the remains had simply been left behind in unmarked graves. Stories of builders turning up human bones on the site of the old prison circulated and some appeared in print.

Contemporary newspaper reports, however, make it clear that when the New Bailey was demolished the remains of the men executed there were transferred to Strangeways Prison and interred in a plot which later received the bodies of a hundred men subsequently executed at Strangeways. In addition, this plot at Strangeways Prison later received the remains of eight men executed at Knutsford Prison, where they were originally buried, before being reburied when that prison closed. There they all remained until the early 1990s.

In the wake of the Strangeways riot of 1990 the interior of the prison was largely rebuilt. The modernisation plans involved building over the area in which the executed were buried. In preparation for this, the bodies were exhumed, cremated and the remains placed in individual canisters. This was done in two stages, first in 1991 and then in

1993. The cremated remains were then buried in two plots, C2710 and C2711, in Blackley Cemetery, North Manchester, purchased by Manchester (HM Prison). Canon Noel Proctor, the former Anglican chaplain of Strangeways prison who, together with another clergyman, supervised the exhumation and re-interment, believes that the remains of the Martyrs are buried in plot C2711.

In 2006 Irish newspapers reported that the Taoiseach, Bertie Ahern, was planning a 'full state funeral for the Manchester Martyrs'. Commentators suggested that such an event would reaffirm Fianna Fáil's republican credentials at a time when Sinn Féin's growing influence in the Republic was calling them into question.

The National Graves Association had by this time traced the remains to Blackley Cemetery. It seemed there was now no obstacle to a state funeral. However, it soon became apparent that because of a failure to record the details of the remains contained in each of the canisters, it is impossible to tell which are those of Allen, Larkin and O'Brien. This oversight has brought to an end the campaign to return the Martyrs to Ireland for burial in Glasnevin Cemetery.

There have always been people in Manchester who have maintained the unbroken tradition of commemoration. In recent years it has assumed a modest form, consisting of the celebration of Mass, in Irish, in the chapel at St Joseph's Cemetery and a procession to the monument, where a group of about thirty say a decade of the Rosary for the repose of the souls of the Martyrs. Many believe that this represents a return to the authentic tradition of the commemoration.

For the foreseeable future the Martyrs will remain in the city with which they will be forever linked, while in Ireland a new generation is hearing the story of the Martyrs for the first time.

***

What is the legacy of the Martyrs?

It is one of the many paradoxes of Irish politics that the memory of the men of violence is most widely invoked when they are safely in their graves and no one is following their example. The Manchester Martyrs, however, occupy a unique position in the nationalist pantheon in that they were the victims of violence, as much as its purveyors. It was common knowledge among Fenians that it was a man named Peter Rice who fired the shot that killed the unfortunate Sergeant Brett. Rice was never arrested and in the aftermath of the rescue made his way to America. He later returned to Ireland and died in Dublin, unremarked, in utter destitution.

Among many nationalists, physical force is now discredited, repudiated even by those who once took up arms. Just as Pearse and Clarke found their inspiration in O'Donovan Rossa, perhaps the new Ireland will find its inspiration in another grave, only a few strides away from the old Fenian's, that of the Martyrs. If the story of the Manchester Martyrs tells us anything, it speaks of the transformative power of suffering. That's why it is perhaps fitting that their grave in Glasnevin should remain empty.

APPENDIX 1

MAIN CHARACTERS, EVENTS AND ORGANISATIONS

Allen, William (1848–1867): one of the Manchester Martyrs, executed with Michael Larkin and Michael O'Brien. Born near Tipperary town. Father a Protestant but Allen converted to Catholicism at the age of fifteen. Apprenticed to a master carpenter and timber merchant in Bandon and spent some time in Dublin as a builder's clerk. Came to Manchester at the end of 1864 looking for work and seems to have travelled backwards and forwards on several occasions. While in Dublin working he met Thomas Kelly and subsequently became one of his key deputies in Manchester.

Barrett, Seamus (dates unknown): noted veteran Manchester Fenian, formed a Manchester Martyrs Memorial Committee at the beginning of the twentieth century which put up the monument in Moston Catholic Cemetery and revived the tradition of an annual commemoration.

Birmingham bombings: 21 November 1974, Provisional IRA planted bombs in Birmingham pubs, killing twenty-one people and injuring 162. At that time the biggest bomb in Britain during the Troubles.

Birmingham Six: Hugh Callaghan, Patrick Joseph Hill, Gerard

Hunter, Richard McIlkenny, William Power and John Walker, sentenced to life imprisonment for the Birmingham bombings; released and received substantial compensation in 1991 when their convictions were declared unsafe.

Bolger (O'Bolger), Thomas (dates unknown): Manchester Fenian who took part in the rescue of Thomas Kelly and Timothy Deasy and escaped arrest. He and Edward Condon later gave differing accounts of the rescue and were clearly antagonistic to each other.

Brett, Charles (1816–1867): police sergeant killed during the rescue of Thomas Kelly and Timothy Deasy and the first Manchester policeman killed in the course of his duty. The commemorative plaque erected in his parish church, St Barnabas', was re-consecrated at St Ann's church, St Ann's Square, Manchester, in 1959, where it remains today. The sergeant's headstone in Harpurhey Cemetery, Manchester has been vandalised.

Brophy, Hugh Francis (1829–1919): a leading Fenian who worked closely with James Stephens; transported for treason on board the last convict ship to Australia, the *Hougoumont*, in 1868.

Calcraft, William (1800–1879): most famous executioner of the nineteenth century who was sixty-seven years old at the time of the Martyrs' execution. He started as a cobbler and became official hangman in 1829. He used a drop of between one and two feet, which critics claimed was not enough to ensure immediate death. Strict churchgoer devoted to his wife and three children and animal lover who gave generously to charity. Devoted to the garden of his Shoreditch home. By 1867 he had a reputation as a bungler. One biographer said, 'At Manchester ... he is said to have shown more signs of weakness than any man put to death.'

Chartists: those who supported the People's Charter demanding fundamental political changes which would have introduced universal male suffrage for parliamentary elections. This and other demands were revolutionary at the time (1838–1850). Chartism is often regarded as one of the first mass political movements. Its opponents saw it as a threat to the established order, an invitation to those without property to interfere in the running of the country and a harbinger of revolution.

Clan na Gael: Irish-American revolutionary organisation formed after the failure of the 1867 rising to bring about an independent Irish republic.

Condon, Edward O'Meagher (1841–1915): tried under the pseudonym Edward Shore and sentenced to death for the murder of Charles Brett. Sentence commuted to penal servitude for life. Released in 1878 from Portland Prison and exiled to America. Employed by the US Post Office. In 1909 he returned to Ireland and received the freedom of Dublin. Visited Manchester, by which time he was associated with John Redmond's Nationalist Party, which alienated Fenians.

Connolly Association (CA): founded in 1938 to 'work for the complete freedom of the Irish people', especially through a united Ireland. The CA's paper, *Irish Freedom*, was first published in January 1939, being renamed the *Irish Democrat* in 1945.

Corydon, John Joseph (dates unknown): born in Liverpool, went to America and fought in the Civil War. Joined the Fenians and was already informing to the British by the time he returned to Ireland in preparation for the 1867 rising. Acted as a despatch messenger between the leaders on both sides of the Atlantic for nearly two years. Gave information about the plan to raid Chester Castle and the Irish rising of 1867. Put the authorities onto Patrick Condon, alias Godfrey Massey, who also became a British agent.

Cullen, Paul (1803–1878): academic, ecclesiastic, rector of Rome's Irish College; archbishop of Armagh and Dublin (1852–1878); opposed Queen's Colleges; opposed clerical involvement in politics and extremely critical of Fenians; Ireland's first cardinal and largely responsible for the structure of the Irish church which survived until the 1980s.

Darragh, Daniel (1836–1870): tried under the pseudonym William Pherson Thompson for acquiring guns for the Manchester rescue. Sentenced to life imprisonment. Died of TB in prison. Exhumed and buried in his native town, Ballycastle, County Antrim, under a monument.

Deasy, Captain Timothy (1839–1880): rescued with Thomas Kelly in Manchester when he was second only to Kelly in the Fenian organisation. Escaped to America. Elected to the city council in Lawrence, Massachusetts in 1870. In 1872 he became one of the first Irish Catholics elected to serve in the Massachusetts House of Representatives.

De Valera, Éamon (1882–1975): dominant political figure in twentieth-century Ireland; took part in the 1916 Easter

Rising; leader in the subsequent War of Independence and of anti-Treaty government in the Irish Civil War; founded Fianna Fáil party and was head of government from 1932 to 1948, 1951 to 1954 and 1957 to 1959; President of Ireland from 1959 to 1973; introduced the Constitution of Ireland.

Denvir, John (1834–1916): born in Bushmills, County Antrim; ran a building firm in Liverpool and later managed and edited there the *Catholic Times*, *United Irishman* and *The Nationalist*; joined the IRB and with Ricard O'Sullivan Burke supplied arms; left the IRB in 1867 and joined the Home Rule movement; elected first secretary of the Home Rule Confederation of Great Britain; most famous for *The Life Story of an Old Rebel* (Dublin 1910).

Derby, Lord (Edward George Geoffrey Smith-Stanley, 14th Earl of Derby) (1799–1869): statesman, three times Conservative prime minister.

Devoy, John (1841–1928): Fenian, imprisoned 1861–1871 and then exiled to the USA where he marshalled support for national revolution; key figure in the Land League and preparation for the 1916 Easter Rising. His posthumously published *Recollections of an Irish Rebel* (1929) is a seminal nationalist work.

Duffy, Edward (*c.*1840–*c.*1868): born in Ballaghadreen, County Mayo. Draper, became a Fenian in 1861 and a full-time operative in 1863. Roles included distributing the *Irish People*, recruiting new members, organisation and training, and he gave classes on Fenian beliefs. Arrested with James Stephens in 1865; released because of ill-health and took part in the 1867 rising; arrested, he was sentenced to fifteen years penal servitude and died in Millbank Prison in 1868.

Emmet, Robert (1778–1803): nationalist orator who led the rebellion against British rule in 1803; captured, tried and executed for high treason. Heroic figure whose speech from the dock is much quoted.

Enniskillen bombing (8 November 1987): an IRA bomb killed eleven at the Enniskillen Remembrance Day service. At least sixty-three people were injured in the blast, nine seriously.

Flood, John (dates unknown): born in Wexford; took part in the rescue of James Stephens from Richmond Gaol and later became head centre for England.

Gadd, Fr Charles Joseph (1838–1907): Irish curate at Salford Cathedral and prison chaplain who ministered to the condemned men daily; later vicar general of Salford; stated 'I never had more devotional penitents in my life than the condemned Irishmen in Salford gaol.'

Gathorne-Hardy, Gathorne (1st Earl of Cranbrook) (1814–1906): prominent Conservative politician; held office in every Conservative government from 1858 to 1892 and was home secretary at the time of the Martyrs' trial.

Guildford Four: at the height of the Troubles, Paul Michael Hill, Gerard Conlon, Patrick Armstrong and Carole Richardson were wrongly convicted for bombing pubs in Guildford in October 1974 when four soldiers and one civilian were killed, whilst a further sixty-five were wounded.

Home Rule: a limited form of Irish independence which would involve the establishment of a parliament in Dublin

responsible for Irish affairs. Power over taxation and foreign
policy would remain under the British crown. This was
similar to the situation which operated in British Dominions
such as Canada. The Home Rule campaign dominated Irish
politics from the 1870s to the outbreak of the Great War.

Hume, John (b. 1937): founding member of the Social
Democratic and Labour Party (SDLP) and received the
Nobel Peace Prize in 1998. Major figure in Northern Irish
politics.

Hunger strikers (1981): Irish republican prisoners who refused
to take food as part of a long-running demand for status as
political prisoners. One hunger striker, Bobby Sands, was
elected MP during the strike, which was called off after ten
had died, including Sands himself. His funeral attracted
100,000 mourners.

Irish Republican Socialist Party: founded in 1974 by former
members of the Official Republican Movement, independent
socialists and trade unionists. Had a paramilitary wing, the
Irish National Liberation Army. Rejects any parliamentary
road to socialism, the Peace Process and the Good Friday
Agreement.

Kelly, Thomas J. (1833–1908): Fenian leader rescued in Man-
chester in 1867; escaped to America and worked in the New
York custom-house. Associated with the IRB in New York.
In 1871, he was secretary to the committee which welcomed
the 'Cuba Five', a group of released Fenian prisoners, to New
York. Buried in Woodlawn Cemetery, NY.

Keogh, William and Sadleir, John: Catholic MPs elected in the

1850s on a pledge that they would mount an 'independent opposition' working for an Irish parliament. Subsequently accepted British government posts and hence regarded as betraying their commitments.

Kickham, Charles (1828–1882): born in County Tipperary, rendered virtually blind and deaf in an accident when he was thirteen years old. Poet and writer. Took part in the 1848 rising, was a founding member of the Fenians and editor of the *Irish People*. He was sentenced to fourteen years' penal servitude for treason in 1865, but released because of ill-health in 1869 and became leader of the Fenians.

Land League: political organisation which worked to help poor tenant farmers, ultimately by getting the British government to allow them to buy the land they worked. Achieved this objective at the beginning of the twentieth century.

Larkin, Michael (1835–1867): born in the parish of Lusmagh, King's County (Offaly); one of the Manchester Martyrs, executed with William Allen and Michael O'Brien; played a part in the administration of one of Manchester's Fenian circles and devoted a great deal of time to the movement. A tailor, he was the only one of the Martyrs who was married, with four children and an aged mother to support. At the time of the rescue he had recently returned from burying his father in Ireland and was unwell.

Luby, Thomas Clarke (1822–1901): founding member of the Fenian Brotherhood, lawyer, author and journalist. He was a member of the Repeal Association – a campaign initiated by Daniel O'Connell to break the union with England and restore an Irish parliament – and a Young Irelander, and wrote for *The Nation*. Arrested with other leading Fenians in 1865, he was convicted of treason-felony and sentenced to twenty years' penal servitude. Amnestied in 1870, he went to the USA where he became a leading figure in Clan na Gael and the Irish Confederation.

M62 bombing: in February 1974 on the M62 motorway in northern England, an IRA bomb exploded on a coach carrying off-duty British soldiers and their families, killing nine soldiers and three civilians. The conviction of Judith Ward in connection with the bombing was later overturned.

Maguire, Thomas (b. 1836): a Royal Marine who had served for ten years and had no Fenian involvement. He had just returned home on leave when he was arrested, tried and sentenced to death for the murder of Sergeant Brett in the rescue of Thomas Kelly and Timothy Deasy. Received a free pardon.

Mallon and Talbot affair: in 1957, Kevin Mallon and Patrick Talbot were arrested in connection with the murder of an RUC officer who was blown up in Coalisland, County Tyrone. There were grave concerns about the way in which the inquiry was conducted and their subsequent conviction and imprisonment. Both men were released at the end of the Border Campaign in 1962.

Massey, Patrick (dates unknown): born in Tipperary town; joined the British army; emigrated to the USA in 1856 and fought for the Confederates in the Civil War; joined the Fenians and had a key role in the 1867 rising; arrested at Limerick Junction and turned informer.

Mayo, Lord (Richard Southwell Bourke, 6th Earl of Mayo) (1822–1872): prominent Conservative politician and three times chief secretary for Ireland – in effect the British government in Ireland.

McCafferty, John (dates unknown): his penchant for violence was confirmed in 1882 when a Fenian splinter group, the Invincibles – an organisation in which he was a leading figure – carried out the infamous Phoenix Park murders.

McHale, John (1791–1881): Catholic Archbishop of Tuam (1834–1881); noted for his concern for the poor; supporter of Daniel O'Connell's Repeal Association – a campaign for the repeal of the Union with England – and tenants' rights, but opposed the Land League.

McManus, Terence Bellew (1823–1860): Young Irelander active in O'Connell's Repeal Association. Fought in the 1848 rising; was deported to Tasmania; escaped to the USA in 1852 where he died. His funeral in Dublin in 1861 was a great propaganda triumph for the Fenians.

Mendis, Viraj (dates unknown): Sri Lankan Communist who sought to avoid extradition by taking sanctuary in the Church of the Ascension in Manchester in 1986. Police raided the church in January 1989 and he was deported to Sri Lanka where, despite dire predictions of his treatment at the hands of a cruel government, he came to no harm.

Mitchel, John (1815–1875): Protestant, solicitor, member of the Repeal Association; became lead writer for *The Nation* and advocate of an independent Irish republic established by revolution; prominent Young Irelander and writer for *United*

Irishman, as a result of which he was convicted of treason-felony and deported to Tasmania; escaped to the USA in 1853; financial agent of the Fenians; returned to Ireland in 1875; elected MP for County Tipperary. His writings, particularly *Jail Journal* (1913), had a profound effect on nationalist thinking.

Murphy, Fr John (1753–1798): Wexford Catholic priest who took part in the fighting during the United Irishmen rising of 1798. Killed in action.

Murphy, Fr Michael (1767–1798): Wexford Catholic priest executed for his part in the fighting during the United Irishmen rising of 1798.

Nagle, Pierce (dates unknown): born near Clonmel, County Tipperary. Spent time in America and on returning to Ireland had odd jobs before securing a position in the print room of Fenian *Irish People*. Provided British authorities with information on preparations for the rising of 1865 and subsequently gave evidence against many leading Fenians convicted in the aftermath.

O'Brien, Michael (1837–1867): one of the Manchester Martyrs, executed with William Allen and Michael Larkin. Born in Ballymacoda, County Cork. Served an apprenticeship as a draper before emigrating to America and serving in the Federal Army during the Civil War. Travelled to Liverpool at the end of the war. Described as a man of 'genteel appearance and attractive manners'.

O'Brien, William Smith (1803–1864): nationalist politician, MP for Ennis, supported Catholic emancipation and later acting leader of the Repeal Association but broke with Daniel O'Connell and was a leader of the rising of 1848. Convicted of high treason and transported to Tasmania. Pardoned in 1854 and later rejected Fenianism.

O'Connell, Daniel (1775–1847): The Liberator, or The Emancipator, dominated Irish politics for the first half of the nineteenth century; campaigned for Catholic Emancipation – the right of Catholics to sit in parliament, etc. – and the Repeal of the Union.

O'Donovan Rossa, Jeremiah (1831–1915): born in Rosscarbery, County Cork. Formed the Phoenix Society, dedicated to breaking the English connection. From then the authorities regarded him as a dangerous revolutionary. Joined the Fenians, managed the Fenian newspaper, the *Irish People*. Trekking the country to promote the paper and win recruits made him a marked man. In September 1865 he was arrested and sentenced to life imprisonment. Suffered great hardship in prison and became the symbol of Ireland's suffering. In 1869 he was elected MP for Tipperary and the Devon Commission was set up to investigate the treatment of Fenian prisoners. Released and went into exile in the USA where he set up the Irish Confederation working for Irish independence.

O'Leary, John (1830–1907): born in Tipperary town; imprisoned for his part in the prison break of those arrested for the 1848 rising and escaped by himself. Financial agent for the Fenians and editor of the *Irish People*. In 1865 he was sentenced to twenty years' penal servitude for high treason, released into exile in 1874. Returned to Ireland in 1885 and became a leading figure in the Irish literary revival.

O'Mahony, John Francis (1816–1877): born in Kilbehenny, County Limerick. He received a good education, devoted his life to freeing Ireland, was a member of the Repeal Association and joined the Young Irelanders. Participated in the insurrection of William Smith O'Brien in 1848, and after its failure fled to France where with James Stephens he devised a new revolutionary organisation. In 1852 he went to New York and there in 1858 was a member of the committee that sent a delegate to Stephens in Dublin with proposals for the founding of the Fenian Brotherhood. One of the most active and influential promoters of the organisation, he was for a time its president. Final years lived in poverty. He died in New York in 1877 and is buried in Glasnevin Cemetery, Dublin. Wrote extensively.

O'Sullivan Burke, Ricard (1838–1922): born in Dunmanway, County Cork. Purveyor of arms for the Fenians. Provided guns for the rescue of Thomas Kelly and Timothy Deasy. Arrested in London in December 1867 and held at Clerkenwell Prison. In an attempt to rescue him an explosion demolished the prison wall, destroyed a number of nearby houses, killed twelve and seriously injured thirty. His health deteriorated during his imprisonment and he was released from a prison for the criminally insane in 1871.

Pan-African Congress: previously a South African liberation movement, now a small political party.

Pearse, Patrick Henry (1879–1916): teacher, barrister, poet, writer, nationalist and political activist. Pearse was spokesman for and the most prominent leader of the 1916 Easter Rising, in which a group of nationalists tried to establish an Irish republic by force of arms; like Tom Clarke, another leading figure in the rising, he was a member of the IRB.

Phoenix Park Murders (1882): a group of nationalist terrorists, the Invincibles, murdered Thomas Burke, the permanent under secretary in the Irish Office, and Lord Cavendish, the chief secretary for Ireland, in Phoenix Park, Dublin; the murders aroused enormous hostility in England and threatened to derail the progress of Parnell's Home Rule Party; the trial attracted worldwide attention as five men – Joe Brady, Daniel Curley, Tim Kelly, Thomas Caffrey and Michael Fagan – were executed, mainly on the evidence of James Carey, one of the leaders of the plot; Carey was subsequently murdered in revenge for his treachery.

Poll Tax (Community Charge): tax introduced by Margaret Thatcher's Conservative government in 1990, replacing the old rating system for local taxation. The new tax was to be paid by all adults, whereas only householders had paid rates. There was widespread opposition to the new system and demonstrations against it resulted in disorder. The tax was eventually withdrawn and the old system restored in all but name.

Prevention of Terrorism Act (1975): act to 'proscribe organisations concerned in terrorism, and to give power to exclude certain persons from Great Britain in order to prevent acts of terrorism, and for connected purposes' which gave the government wide powers of arrest. Many regarded it as repressive.

Rice, Peter (dates unknown): although he was never arrested, both Edward Condon and John Devoy claim that he fired the shot that killed Charles Brett. This fits in with William Allen's adamant assertion, right to the end, that someone else, who was not captured, had fired the shot.

Roberts, William Randall (1830–1897): born in County Cork, leading American Fenian and, in 1865, president of the Fenian Society; behind the Fenian raid into Canada in 1866. Later elected to the House of Representatives.

Roche, Fr Philip (1760–1798): Wexford Catholic priest who took part in the fighting during the United Irishmen rising of 1798.

Sadleir, John: see Keogh, William.

Stephens, James (1824–1901): born in Kilkenny. Co-founder of the Fenian movement with John O'Mahony in 1858 and its driving force for many years. Apprentice railway engineer. Fought in the 1848 rebellion and fled to France. Ousted by the leaders of the 1867 rising. Lived in exile until 1891 when he returned to retire quietly in Dublin. Present at the unveiling of the monument to the Manchester Martyrs in St Joseph's Cemetery, 1908.

Sullivan, A. M. (Alexander Martin) (1830–1884): editor of *The Nation*, Home Rule MP and QC. With his brother, T. D. Sullivan he made *The Nation* a leading Irish nationalist newspaper. Played a major role in organising the Manchester Martyrs' commemoration in Dublin in 1867 and was imprisoned for inflammatory newspaper articles about it. Major temperance figure.

Sullivan, T. D. (Timothy Daniel) (1827–1914): brother of A. M. Sullivan. Nationalist, journalist and Home Rule MP; author of the song 'God Save Ireland'. Owned several nationalist newspapers, was briefly imprisoned for his writing; lord mayor of Dublin, 1886 and 1887.

Tone, Theobald Wolfe (1763–1798): key figure in the United Irishmen movement which sought the establishment of an independent Irish republic by force of arms. With support from revolutionary France he led a military rising in 1798 which the British suppressed with great brutality. Tone died in prison shortly after the rising. He was a seminal figure in Irish republicanism.

Young Ireland: political and cultural movement of the mid-nineteenth century which promoted nationalism and led to the rebellion of 1848. Many leaders were sentenced to transportation. Had great influence on subsequent nationalist thinking.

APPENDIX 2

'GOD SAVE IRELAND', T. D. SULLIVAN

Chorus:

God save Ireland, said the heroes

God save Ireland, said they all

Whether on the scaffold high

Or the battlefield we die

Oh what matter when for Erin dear we fall?

High upon the gallows tree

Swung the noble hearted three

By the vengeful tyrant stricken in their bloom

But they met him face to face

With the courage of their race

And they went with souls undaunted to their doom

Chorus

When they're up the rugged stair

Rang their voices out in prayer

Then with England's fatal cord around them cast

Close beside the gallows tree
Kissed like brothers lovingly
True to home and faith and freedom to the last

Chorus

Never till the latest day
Shall the memory pass away
Oh, the gallant lives thus given for our land
But on the cause must go
Amid joy and weal and woe
Till we make our Isle a nation free and grand

Chorus

APPENDIX 3

'THE SMASHING OF THE VAN' /
'THE MANCHESTER MARTYRS',
STREET BALLAD, AUTHOR UNKNOWN

Attend you gallant Irishmen and listen for a while
I'll sing to you the praises of the sons of Erin's Isle
It's of those gallant heroes who voluntarily ran
To release two Irish Fenians from an English prison van.
On the eighteenth of September, it was a dreadful year,
When sorrow and excitement ran throughout all Lancashire,
At a gathering of the Irish boys they volunteered each man,
To release those Irish prisoners out of the prison van.
Kelly and Deasy were their names, I suppose you knew them
    well,
Remanded for a week they were in Bellevue Gaol to dwell,
When taking of the prisoners back, their trial for to stand,
To make a safe deliverance they conveyed them in a van.
William Deasy was a man of good and noted fame,
Likewise Michael Larkin, we'll never forget his name,
With young Allen and O'Brien they took a part so grand,
In that glorious liberation and the smashing of the van.
In Manchester one morning those heroes did agree,
Their leaders, Kelly and Deasy, should have their liberty,

They drank a health to Ireland, and soon made up the plan,

To meet the prisoners on the road and take and smash the van.

With courage bold those heroes went and soon the van did stop,

They cleared the guards from back and front and then smashed in the top,

But in blowing open of the lock, they chanced to kill a man,

So three must die on the scaffold high for smashing of the van.

One cold November morning in eighteen sixty-seven

These martyrs to their country's cause a sacrifice were given,

'God save Ireland', was the cry, all through the crowd it ran,

The Lord have mercy on the boys that helped to smash the van.

So now kind friends I will conclude, I think it would be right

That all true-hearted Irishmen together should unite,

Together should sympathise, my friends, and do the best we can

To keep the memories ever green of the boys that smashed the van.

APPENDIX 4

The Fenian Proclamation

We have suffered centuries of outrage, enforced poverty, and bitter misery. Our rights and liberties have been trampled on by an alien aristocracy, who treated us as foes, usurped our lands, and drew away from our unfortunate country all material riches. The real owners of the soil were removed to make room for cattle, and driven across the ocean to seek the means of living, and the political rights denied to them at home, while our men of thought and action were condemned to loss of life and liberty. But we never lost the memory and hope of a national existence. We appealed in vain to the reason and sense of justice of the dominant powers. Our mildest remonstrances were met with sneers and contempt. Our appeals to arms were always unsuccessful.

Today, having no honourable alternative left, we again appeal to force as our last resource. We accept the conditions of appeal, manfully deeming it better to die in the struggle for freedom than to continue an existence of utter serfdom.

All men are born with equal rights, and in associating to protect one another and share public burdens, justice demands that such associations should rest upon a basis which maintains equality instead of destroying it.

We therefore declare that, unable longer to endure the curse of Monarchical Government, we aim at founding a Republic based on universal suffrage, which shall secure to all the intrinsic value of their labour.

The soil of Ireland, at present in the possession of an oligarchy, belongs to us, the Irish people, and to us it must be restored.

We declare, also, in favour of absolute liberty of conscience, and complete separation of Church and State.

We appeal to the Highest Tribunal for evidence of the justness of our cause. History bears testimony to the integrity of our sufferings, and we declare, in the face of our brethren, that we intend no war against the people of England – our war is against the aristocratic locusts, whether English or Irish, who have eaten the verdure of our fields – against the aristocratic leeches who drain alike our fields and theirs.

Republicans of the entire world, our cause is your cause. Our enemy is your enemy. Let your hearts be with us. As for you, workmen of England, it is not only your hearts we wish, but your arms. Remember the starvation and degradation brought to your firesides by the oppression of labour. Remember the past, look well to the future, and avenge yourselves by giving liberty to your children in the coming struggle for human liberty.

Herewith we proclaim the Irish Republic.

The Provisional Government.

BIBLIOGRAPHY

Akenson, Donal Harman, *The Irish Diaspora: a primer*, Belfast 1996

Campbell, Christopher, *Fenian Fire: the British Government plot to assassinate Queen Victoria*, London 2003

Cashman, Denis B., *Fenian Diary* (edited and introduced by C. W. Sullivan III), Dublin 2001

Comerford, R. V., *The Fenians in Context: Irish politics and society, 1848–82*, Dublin 1998

Connolly, S. J., *The Oxford Companion to Irish History*, Oxford 2011

Coogan, Tim Pat, *Wherever Green is Worn: the story of the Irish Diaspora*, London 2002

Curtis, Liz, *The Cause of Ireland – from the United Irishmen to Partition*, Belfast 1994

Denieffe, Joseph, *A Personal Narrative of the Irish Revolutionary Brotherhood* (introduction by Seán Ó Lúing), Shannon 1969

Denvir, John, *The Life Story of an Old Rebel*, Dublin 1910

Devoy, John, *Recollections of an Irish Rebel*, New York 1929

Doughty, Jack, *The Manchester Outrage – a Fenian tragedy*, Oldham 2001

Elliott, Marianne, *The Catholics of Ulster*, New York 2001

Engels, Friedrich, *The Condition of the Working Class in England*, London 1969

English, Richard, *Irish Freedom: a history of nationalism in Ireland*, London 2007

Glynn, Anthony, *High Upon the Gallows Tree: the story of the Manchester Fenian rescue of 1867 and of Allen, Larkin and O'Brien*, Tralee 1967

Golway, Terry, *For the Cause of Liberty: a thousand years of Ireland's heroes*, London 2000

Herbert, Anthony, *The Wearing of the Green – a political history of the Irish in Manchester*, London 2011

Jenkins, B., *The Fenian Problem: insurgency and terrorism in a liberal state, 1858–1874*, Liverpool 2009

Kee, Robert, *The Green Flag*, Harmondsworth 1989

Keneally, Thomas, *The Great Shame: a story of the Irish in the Old World and the New*, London 1998

Mitchel, John, *Jail Journal*, London 1913

Moloney, Ed, *A Secret History of the IRA*, London 2007

Moody, T. W. and Martin, F. X., *The Course of Irish History*, new revised edition, Cork 2011

Ó Broin, Leon, *Fenian Fever: an Anglo-American dilemma*, London 1971

O'Connor, Kevin, *The Irish in Britain*, Dublin 1974

O'Dea, John, *The Story of the Old Faith in Manchester*, London 1910

O'Donovan Rossa, Jeremiah, *Rossa's Recollections, 1838–1898* (introduction by Seán Ó Lúing), Shannon 1972

O'Leary, John, *Recollections of Fenians and Fenianism* (Vols I and II), Shannon 1969

O'Neill, Joseph, *Crime City: Manchester's Victorian underworld*, Milo 2008

O'Sullivan, Patrick, *The Irish World Wide – patterns of migration*, Leicester 1992

Ramón, Marta, *A Provisional Dictator: James Stephens and the Fenian Movement*, Dublin 2007

Rose, Paul, *The Manchester Martyrs, the story of a Fenian tragedy*, London 1970

Ryan, Desmond, *The Fenian Chief: a biography of James Stephens, with an introductory memoir by Patrick Lynch*, Dublin 1967

Shaw, A. G. L., *Convicts and Colonies: a study of penal transportation from Great Britain and Ireland to Australia and other parts of the British Empire*, Melbourne 1977

Townshend, Charles, *Political Violence in Ireland: government and resistance since 1848*, Oxford 1983

Papers of the Manchester Martyrs Commemoration Committee, and other items accumulated over decades relating to the Martyrs, in the Linen Hall Library, Belfast

JOURNALS FROM THE PERIOD COVERED

Daily Telegraph	*Manchester Examiner*
Freeman's Journal, The	*Manchester Guardian, The*
Illustrated London News, The	*Manchester Weekly Times*
Irish People	*Police Gazette, The*
Irish Times, The	*Reynold's News, The*
Manchester Courier, The	*Sunday Chronicle*
Manchester Evening Chronicle, The	*Times, The*

INDEX